IT'S NE
LATE

MW00592328

"Vetena"

IT'S NEVER TOO LATE

BY

ViTINA CORSO GULINO

www.bookstandpublishing.com

Published by
Bookstand Publishing
Morgan Hill, CA 95037
3177_4

Copyright © 2010 by ViTina Corso Gulino
All rights reserved. No part of this publication may be
reproduced or transmitted in any form or by any means,
electronic or mechanical, including photocopy, recording,
or any information storage and retrieval system, without
permission in writing from the copyright owner.

ISBN 978-1-58909-765-0

Printed in the United States of America

Who are we to say when Life is taken away?
Another time,
Another place
Memories left
behind, for all to
share.
The gentle touch of
holding hands
Taking in what God
has given us
The color of the
changing seasons
The many problems
we solved together
The many precious
dreams that came
true
Love of long Life together, the love we gave
These are all the beautiful Memories
I will keep within my Heart forever more.

ViTina

DEDICATION

This book is dedicated to my two daughters

My baby boomers, Angela and Nancy

And their husbands Ray and Joe

Who became My Sons

ACKNOWLEDGMENTS

- To all the people that were part of this book, and inspired me when I thought, who would want to know about someone else's Life. They all came through my life and left an imprint on me.

- To my family whom were always there when I needed them, and encouraged me to finish the book. My daughter Angela, who always knew when I was depressed or frustrated and came to my rescue and solved any problem that came up with the book. She took over and edited it.

- Friends, who always asked ("how is the book coming") along and couldn't wait till it was finished.

- My Grandmother, Vitina who will always be part of me till the end.

- My Mother and Father, who taught me about life's good and bad times. Frankie, my baby brother who I took care of when he was born and I always remembered how close we were to each other.

- My Godson Ludwig (Luddy) Guarino who did all the research of the Corso and Alogna Families.

- Luddy's Sister Anne who gave me some advice on how she published her book. She published a cook book called "Growing Up Italian", of all the Sicilian recipes and always called to talk to me. (Anne Marie Guarino-Schrank)

- To William R. Snyder ll, the young man who loved printing most of the pictures in the book.

- Mike and Maria Lecesse, the people that gave me the courage to stay in college, get my degree and are my dear friends.

- Cressa Moran from the Washington Irving Senior Center in Catskill, New York, who helped prepare the book for publication. I couldn't have done it without her. She also typed some of my chapters when my fingers were hurting from arthritis or when I thought I lost what I wrote on the computer.

- Andrew and Ann Marston friends of my grandchildren Tina and Chris had mentioned to them that I couldn't get my manuscript printed because it was on a different software Andrew took a few minutes to fix it and I got the manuscript printed. As you can guess I am not a computer expert.

- Chanelle a Photo Specialist in Myrtle Beach made the sizes of some pictures for the book. For all the people who help with this book and touch my Life and you know who you are, I Thank You.

- Last, but certainly not least, my Grandson James, who had the patience with me when I would screw up the computer or had a word that I couldn't spell finished the book, going over line by line to correct my grammar; I never could have done it without him.

It's Never Too Late

Old age is an adventure with no commitments

only what

you want to do the rest of your Life.

CONTENTS

PREFACE

I really haven't the foggiest idea of where or how to start this book. Having been married for over 50 years, it is unbelievable to reflect upon what my LIFE is all about. How does one go about telling all the things they have done? Well here goes, and some of the things, that standout in my Life.

I have had five careers and treated each one as a challenge.

The first, career started when I had to drop out of school at sixteen. It was during the time of the Depression and my mother had another baby. She left me in charge of my three week old baby brother Frankie, while she went back to work. I took care of him until he was almost two.

My second, career was in the garment industry. I worked in it for twenty four years. There was no future in this job, it was a sweat shop. I left when Mayor La-Guardia started to send work out of the country.

The third, career was in school food service, I enjoyed the work and most of all, the students. D.C.37, our Food Service Union made me an offer which I couldn't refuse, to go to college and get an Applied Science Degree in Food Service Management. It was almost like winning the Lottery only better because they paid for it.

The fourth, career was an offer as a Para-professional at Richmond Hill High School. This is when my interest in Special -Education reached a new level. *I was in charge of a new program for special ed. students in school food service.* The students within this program received one credit for the terms training. With my prior experience in food service and my expertise I gave the students valuable training to compete for jobs in the Food Service Field. One of my students upon graduation received a job as a food service worker.

The fifth, career, I applied for a job as a Substitute teacher at the Catskill School District in March of 1988. I was only going to work two days a week, but ended up over one hundred days in a term. It has been nineteen years and I was still subbing until I took my name off the list in August of 2007 at age 83.

Chapter One

NOW MY STORY BEGINS

The Immigration of My Family

1904 The Corso Families

My fathers' and mothers' families all landed on Ellis Island in the early 1900 hundreds. Grandpa Corso, my paternal grandfather was the first to come in April 13, 1904 with his younger brother.

The Victoria

Associated Passenger	Date of Arrival	Port of Departure
Corso, Giuseppe	April 13, 1904	Palermo

Built by Robert Duncan & Company, P..
Scotland, 1872. 3,358 gross tons; 36(
long; 40 feet wide. Compound engine,
screw. Service speed 12 knots. 1,43(
passengers (150 first class, 80 second
1,200 third class).

Built for Anchor Line, British flag, in 1t
named **Victoria**. Glasgow-New York a
Bombay service. Later Mediterranean-
service. Scrapped in Italy in 1905.

Photo: Laurence Dunn Collection

Associated Passenger
Milazzo, Vita

Date of Arrival
Sep 02, 1905

Port of Departure
Palermo

Built by Scott's Shipbuilding & Engineering Company, Greenock, Scotland, 1889. 2,900 gross tons; 363 (bp) feet long; 42 feet wide. Compound engines, twin screw. Service speed 12 knots. 1,175 passengers (25 first class, 1,150 third class).

Built for Portugese Government, in 1889 and named **Rei De Portugal**. Sold to Prince Line, in 1902 and renamed **Napolitan Prince**. Mediterranean-New York service. Sold in 1911 and renamed **Manouba**. Marseilles-North Africa service. Compagnie de Navigation Mixte line. Scrapped in Italy in 1929.

Photo: World Ship Society

My Dad who was the oldest child, born in 1897 and was only 8 years old when he came over with his mother and three sisters in 1905.

They lived in a three room tenement apartment in Brooklyn. Dad went to school and graduated from Junior High. His ambition was to become a doctor but of course money was the obstacle. At that time two more boys were born. The family left New York and went to Pennsylvania where there was work in the coal mines. My dad was only 14 and worked with my grandfather in the mines. They were there only six months when there was an accident in the mines. At this time my grandmother told my grandfather that she wasn't going to lose her boys in the mines, so they left Pennsylvania and went back to New York.

Grandfather and my dad worked digging holes for the telephone company in New York to place the telephone poles. Thru the Sicilian grape-vine many of the families heard that there was a new highway being built, between Brooklyn and Queens. They heard that land was being sold near the highway and most of the Corso family bought land in Ozone Park, Queens. Most of the family bought one lot, but grandfather bought four lots. My father in 1920 bought one lot, his two sisters who were married bought one lot each also. My father whom was the oldest and his father soon were building a house for the family. They also built five other houses for my aunts and uncles who were getting married. In those days the families stuck together, near each other. All the houses were on the same road and most were the same, built of blocks and white stucco on the outside just like in the old country.

Grandpa's house was built more of the American style, made of wood and sidings. It had a giant living room with a small kitchen, a toilet and a big wine cellar. He had about eight wine barrels in the place. Of course that was the most important room in the house. The second floor had a bathroom and all the bedrooms, one big room for the boys, barracks style. The girl's room for only one of my aunts had a small closet and a big oblong mirror.

As time went on and the family grew, my father became a mailman and made $25 a week. Everyone considered that a professional big government job at that time.

1916-1918 The Alogna Family

My Maternal Grandmother Mama Anna as we called her was a Widower and left with eight children: Two sons, Iggy and Joe, five daughters, Josephine, Nancy (my mother), Antoinette, Nashua and Mary and one that passed away.

The Patria

ADD TO YOUR ELLIS ISLAND FILE

Associated Passenger	Date of Arrival	Port of Departure
Maglie, Anna	Dec 26, 1916	Palermo

Built by Chantiers de la Mediterranee, La Seyn France, 1913. 11,885 gross tons; 512 (bp) fee long; 59 feet wide. Steam triple expansion engines, twin screw. Service speed 1 knots. 2,240 passengers (140 first class, 25 second class, 1,850 third class).

Built for Fabre Line, French flag, in 1913 and named **Patria**. Mediterranean-New York servic Salvaged and scrapped in 1952.

Photo: Richard Faber Collection

Her father was a traveling delivery-man. He would travel to each country and sometimes to Northern Africa. At the age of thirty eight he had an accident and broke his knee cap. Those days they didn't have the knowledge of treatment for it, and he developed an infection and passed away. Grandmother was left to raise her children alone.

The oldest son Ignacio (Iggy) became the disciplinarian of the family. He took on the role of the

4

father. All decisions were his to make. He would make sure that all the children towed the line. My mother would say he handed out sentences according to how he would feel.

If they were not carried out to his satisfaction the consequence was a beating with a leather strap. Wise to his ways mom gave him no cause to beat her. She always did her chores and then her sewing. She loved to have nice things and designed and sewed her own clothes. This was a talent which came in handy at a later time.

Things weren't going too well in Italy and her two boys were going to be called into the Italian Army. My grandmother decided to send her two sons, who were the oldest, to America to find jobs and a place to live. They arrived here in1916 and found work in constructions jobs. New York was growing by leaps and bounds. They both lived in a tenement on Troutman Street in Brooklyn.

After about a year the boys sent for my grandmother Anna and the rest of the family. I remember my mother telling me as a little girl how when they came over on the boat in 1918, the Captain painted the hull of the boat a different color so that Germany Submarines would think the boat was from a neutral country and they would not be bombed. It was the time of the First World War. It was an experience she would never forget. People slept on the decks and any place else they could find. They ate hard bread and cheese and maybe sometimes spaghetti. It took over two weeks to arrive at Elias Island and my two Uncles, Joe and Iggy, as I remember what we called them by name; met them at the pier. The family had no idea what they had ahead for them. It wasn't easy to begin in a new country.

At that time New York was growing and there was lots of work but very little pay. What helped my grandmother's family were their eight children that went to work. The two boys were working at night in construction so they had the day to sleep and the rest of them, my mother and sisters worked in a factory sewing men's pants during the day. They also took home work at night to make extra money. The whole family worked together. Their dream came true when they bought land in Ozone Park where the Corso Family bought their land. The Alogna Family also built their houses just a few roads apart.

(Mom pictured lower right side)

Today we have the same thing happening with people that want to find the America dream. They don't realize that when our grandparents came here the sacrifice they made in their life and never understanding what it took to survive and sacrifice to be an American. It took Guts.

Chapter Two

1923 The House My Father Started to Build
1924 How He Met My Mother

The story that was told to me growing up was Dad saw my mother when she was going to work. He was building his house at the time and she had to pass that way to go to work. He asked his father if he knew her family and would he find out if he could see her. In those days a boy didn't approach the girl. There were certain rituals that had to be respected and approved by both the families. There was a thorough investigation. Some of the rules were etched in Stone.

- Was it a good family?
- Did they have money?
- Was she healthy?
- Did she know how to cook?
- Could she have children, (especially a male child) so that the father's name would continue?

After a long investigation the families agreed that there would be a marriage. My mother was only seventeen and my father was twenty seven. The only obstacle was my mother really didn't want to get married, but had no say in the arrangement. She only agreed because my father was a mailman and made twenty five dollars a week. She considered that since he had a government job she would be fine.

They were married on April, 23 1923.

As Life would have it, they were married 50 years with many ups and downs as the years went on.

(Below is My Mother and Father)

The First Years of My Life 1924 to 1929

My Birth as told by my mother and paternal grandmother Mama Vitina whom I was named after her. My birth name Vita in Latin means "Life"; in the Sicilian language I was called Vitina, as most of the family would call me. When I graduated elementary school I dropped the VI-and used Tina as my official name.

On a Wednesday my mother started to have contractions at 5:30 that morning. The word went out to all my aunts and both of my grandmothers to come over to the house. In those days they all helped with a birth of a baby. It seemed that my life started with a problem, I wasn't in the right position in the birth canal and all my aunts, and grandmothers could be of no help. Dad decided to call the doctor and explained to him it was an emergency. (In those day doctors would come to the house no matter what time it would be). When he arrived he told my father that he could only save my mother or the baby, as I was a breech baby. As faith would have it in the last minute I decided to turn in my mother's womb and was born feet first on March 19 1924 at 9:30 A.M. on St. Joseph's, Day a very important day in the Catholic religion.

This was the start of another problem. My mother developed a cyst in one of her breasts, so she was unable to nurse me. They gave me fresh cow's milk but I was allergic and lost weight because of this. I guess I wouldn't be here if it wasn't for an Italian doctor who told my mother to feed me barley water. She would boil the barley in water and put the water in my bottle. As I got older she would strain the barley and feed me barley as cereal. The other source of my diet was rice cereal and the renown,

9

cod liver oil. I didn't realize until I was two how it tasted and refused to take it. Mom, found another product called "Scotts Emulsion" with a flavor of Vanilla in it. This was given to me thru out my entire school life.

The children of today have a choice of all the medication and *vitamins and food that makes it fun to take and eat.*

Born in the worst time in history, the beginning of the great depression, I was the lucky one not to realize what the word depression met until later on when it was time to go school. Within that time frame two more sisters were born, Anna on December 9 1925 and Jeanie on July 12 1928. Being the first born it was only natural that I became mother's little helper.

At the time, President Hoover was in office and promised a chicken in every pot but Mom said there was no chicken in any pot. We ate mostly pasta with greens from grandfather's vegetable garden, and all kinds of beans. Dad of course had his meat. I remember a time when I was older, when mom cut a cube of meat for us from his plate, he got so angry and he turned the table upside down.

Things at home were getting to a point that money was a problem and mom had to limit what things we asked for. We all had one pair of shoes for every day and for Sunday they were polished for Sunday's Mass.

She was a seamstress and made all our clothes which saved a lot for three girls. Still money was not enough so she decided that she would go back to work and supplement the family's income. She put the three of us in a day care. Yes, we did have some sort of day care at that time. There were women that took in children for a small fee. The only thing my sister Anna and I remembered about the day care was the lunch they would serve us. My favorite to this day was mash potatoes and carrots with real butter. I still remember the taste and the smell to this day there is nothing that takes the place of butter.

With all the modern changes in the food groups I wonder how butter became a no-no. Maybe one of these days they will find that butter will be taken off the bad food list.

One special time comes to mind, I was three years old when mom had been busy, and she asked me to go down the road to the county store for bread and milk. I was busy playing with my doll. I loved trying to make clothes for my doll. Mom was a seamstress and I would always watch her when she was sewing our dresses. This time I was so engrossed with my doll that I said, NO.

Well, she told my father and he asked me to go. I refused again. He was fixing the inner tube of the baby carriage (in those days the tires had inner tubes) in the wheels. He didn't realize when he swung the tube that he hit my pinky finger. This really wasn't abuse, he was actually so sorry that he hurt me. I never said no again when asked to do something.

Some Facts About My Paternal Grandmother

Mama Vitina, my father's mother lived on the same road, where my father built his house. She also was there when I was born. I grew up most of life with the influence of Mama Vitina. She believed in education and made certain that her children went to school. In those days the women went to work in the garment industries but her boys went to school. My father became a postman, and my Uncles Mike, Dominick and Bill all became policemen. *We still have policemen in the family.*

She had the wisdom of the best psychiatrist and any midwives. She was there for many women who were giving birth and needing help for bringing their children into the world. In those days women depended on each other for their needs. There were no doctors to call because there was very little money available, her only payment was that she wanted that each child be baptized.

I remember when she would find god parents to baptize the baby's. My cousin Rocky and I were godparents to three of the babies. We had to be sixteen to be qualified and needed the permission of the Church. She had a love for people that had less than her. Many a time, if she knew someone that needed food, she would make a pot of soup or greens and beans and send me to the person's house with the hot food.

Mama Vitina taught me how to cook the cuisine of Sicily. These recipes of the old world were handed down from generations from women before her. Grandpa Corso had a big garden and grew all kinds of vegetables and herbs. He had of course, two fig trees, also apple, pears, plums trees and a chestnut tree. Grandma could make a dinner from all the vegetables and fruits from the garden. She also made her own bread and pasta. One of her favorite recipes was made with the flower of the zucchini plant. According to grandpa, did you know that this plant has a male and female flower? The female flower as it grows has a little node at the end of stem, the male has none. These are the ones that are picked to use in the recipe. I don't remember how she made the batter but I later when I was married, that Bisquick is what I used in the recipe. The problem today is that, getting the flowers of the plant is impossible to find unless you grow your own plants. Grandpa Corso always had zucchini plants in his garden.

*Zucchini Flower recipe

12 zucchini flowers.

2 cups of Bisquick.

1 tsp of dry Good Seasons of Salad Dressing.

Oil for frying.

Add 1 tsp of good seasons to the bisquick flour and make a batter according to the box... Dip the flowers in the batter and fry in 2 inches of hot oil.

Sometimes I put shrimp inside the flower before I fry it.

When I wanted to get away after doing what my mother needed done I would escape to grandmother's house.

Aunt Gertie and Uncle Bill were the two adults that were not married. Uncle Bill was sixteen years older than me so I grew up with him. He became my big brother and looked after me,* *even when he got married.* He loved the way I would shine his shoes and iron his shirts, he didn't like the way grandmother did them.

Aunt Gertie went to work in the garment industry. She also liked how I ironed her pleated skirts. I really didn't mind doing the ironing because I loved being with her. She had beautiful clothes, perfume and make up which sometimes she put some on me. She was twenty years older than me.

(Aunt Gertie)

(I was a Flower Girl)

Her wedding took place at grandmother's house. In those days most weddings were at the home.

I also remember that funerals also took place in the home. Most took three days of the family staying up day and night with the deceased.

Some Special Facts

Our Holidays were always special at Grandpa and Grandma's house. Grandpa built the house and made sure that the dining room was large enough for all his children and grandchildren. There was a banquet table large enough for all the adults and a smaller one for seating all his children and grandchildren. There wasn't any other furniture except two rockers and a big radio they listened to when they were alone.

When we entered my grandparents' house we had to give a special greeting. Bless you in Sicilian *"the ssa"*, *"Benidriccu" grandpa would than return the blessing with words "Santa e riccu" meaning in English " May you be blessed and rich".*

This greeting was also used as a blessing of the house and also of the people in it. If we forgot to say the greeting we were sent home, for we didn't show respect to our grandparents.

Also we had to say it in the Sicilian language. We were all unaware that we were learning a different custom and language. How shrewd of my grandparents to insist that we had to learn their language. (* Late in life and in my travels to Italy and Sicily the language was still in my subconscious.)

Most young children pick up the language when they are forced to communicate with their elders. *Just a thought, a foreign language should be taught in elementary school. They are more receptive to learning. When they are in the higher grades they have curriculum to deal with and of course their hormones are jumping.*

Most International countries have a greeting when they enter their homes and of their grandparents home.

In the Jewish Faith they have a similar custom. It is called a mezuzah. The mezuzah is a small little case which contains a scroll hand written to remind them of the presence of God. This is posted by the doorway of the person's home to kiss for they believe in the presence of God in their homes. In my career I worked for a Jewish firm for eighteen years and they became part of my extended family. We exchanged many events of both families. I learned how to eat their food and attended most of the family events, and sometimes went to their Temple. *Most of my life I have had friends whom I have cherished till today.*

Chapter Three

Holidays with the Corso Clan

On the holidays all of children and grandchildren went to our grandparent's house. I remember the excitement of helping my grandmother preparing the food for the whole family. I knew all about most of the food that she would serve because we both planned it. It was always fresh food made from scratch and from grandpa's garden, and the dinner was from soup to nuts. Most of my cousins had no idea what grandma Vitina and I had planned, because they only came around on special holidays but I saw grandma every day. The dessert was my favorite that grandma especially made only on the holidays. I don't remember the Sicilian name for them but I remember how to make them, I have made them every Christmas for the past fifty years.

Vitina's Fig Cookies

2- Rings of Kalamata figs.

Cut off the top stem of the figs with kitchen shears.

½ cup raisins.

½ cup of shelled filberts.

½ cup of shelled almonds.

1 cup orange juice.

1 cup of honey.

1 lemon skin.

1 orange skin.

1 teaspoon almond extract.

Grind figs, raisins, filberts, almonds, lemon and orange.

Add orange juice, honey and almond extract to the above mixture and mix well.

Put in a bowl, cover and refrigerated until you make the pastry.

Pastry for fig cookies.

4cups sifted flour.

1 cup sugar.

1 cup of unsalted butter.

5 egg yolk save the whites for later.

Sift flour sugar cut in butter evenly through add one egg yolk at a time and add milk as needed, knead into 2 balls. Roll pastry between wax paper about 12 in long and 6in wide cut 3 inch strips and roll fig mixture in a rope about one inch in diameter and put in the strips, and seal with beaten egg whites. Bush the tops also with the egg whites and sprinkles. Cut diagonally

Bake in oven 350 degrees until slightly brown.

The Fun Began

After dinner all my cousins and I first had to help grandma and my aunts clean up and do the dishes.

The rest of the day was when the fun began. There was dancing and singing and Grandpa said that all the grandchildren had to participate in an amateur hour.

I remember the many times we went on holidays, Grandpa would be playing the guitar, my father the accordion, Uncle Don, Banjo and Uncle Mike the violin. Most of my cousins had beautiful voices; I of course could not carry a tune, *which I still can't.*

Wine Making Time

In the fall of the year it was a very special time in the Corso Clan. The boxes of grapes were stacked high in the wine cellar and the grape crusher was put on top of the empty whiskey barrel. I really can't say where grandpa got the barrels but to him they had to be special barrels.

Just like the grape, only three special kinds, black, red and green. Most of the time he let us turn the handle on the crusher until we would get tired. He would alternate which color grape he would put in the crusher. After all the grapes were crushed it had to ferment for a number of days in the whiskey barrels. The next procedure was the squeezing of the grape. *This was a wooden cylinder that had a handle that had to be turned so that the pure juice would go into the new whiskey barrels.*

Vino Cotto-*(Cooked Wine)*

Muscat grape which was the sweetest grape and never needed sugar added to the juice and Grandma would add small strips of orange zest spices, cloves and cinnamon sticks boiled it on medium heat to make syrup. When the syrup is reduced by three quarters grandma would remove the spires and put the syrup in tightly sealed jars. She would put them in the ice box which would be used for future desserts.

Cassadedde with Ricotta (Old Sicilian Treat)

The cassadedde pastry was shaped like a turnover only with a mixture of ricotta and the sweet wine syrup inside the pastry.

3 cups flour.

3/4 cup butter.

1 cup ricotta.

1/2 cup sugar.

1 egg.

Ricotta Filling.

Do this first, in a bowl make sure that most of the ricotta fluid is strained. Very important! Then add sugar, egg, half teaspoon of cinnamon, (optional vino cotto) or any flavored fruit Jam.

Soften butter at room temperature add in flour and mix dough with your hands, add milk and continue to knead until it doesn't stick to hands or the bowl. Roll dough about ½ in. thick and make round disks and make a well in the middle put the ricotta filling about a tablespoon in each. My grandmother liked to make the square about 3 inches and then she would fill and fold them like a turnover. Both would be baked in oven of 200 degree for 20 minutes.

The odor of the fresh wine would be in grandpa's house for weeks. Grandpa's wine was very special and known to everyone who made wine. It was the purest and clearest wine made. When he thought by a certain time that the wine was ready to be tapped he would pour some in a glass and bring it to the light; it had to be as clear as the color of pure (Garnet) then he knew that it was time to seal the barrels top to age. His wine cellar was run like some of the best wine cellars of today. Many of his neighbors would come to get his wine for a price. I never found out how much he charged for a gallon.

Chapter Four

Now Back to My Life

1929-1938

Finally I was five years old and started kindergarten. Going to school was the only time that I didn't have to take care of my sisters all day. When I came home from school my job was still taking care of my sisters we would play with our dolls or I would read nursery rhymes to them. Sometimes they would be sleeping and that would give me time to sew a dress for my doll. Of course my mother needed me to do something else. I felt that every time she would have another chore for me to do. One day after I went to bed she put my doll and her clothes in the coal bin. In those days there was a room in the basement where the coal man would put the coal through a window with a shoot into the bin.

In the morning I asked mom where my doll was, she told me that I would get it back only if I did what she asked me to do, I promised. What she didn't know was I had seen her bring my doll to the basement.

At this time my world started to change, I loved going to school. There were so many things to do and learn. My kindergarten teacher was Mrs. Springer (not her real name) she was so patient and loving with all of her students. I loved when she read to us and made everything seem so real. In those days the grades went from kindergarten to eighth grade. Our dress code was a navy skirt, white cotton blouse with a sailor collar and a red tie. Oh yes, I remember the first boy that I liked in class, his name was Charlie Silver. To me, he seemed like he came from a rich family and was the only one driven to school every day. We went thru the eighth grade and he didn't even know I existed.

My favorite subjects were Home Economics, Reading and Geography; I wanted to find the places my family came from. Just, maybe someday I would go visit the country. *(Even at that young age I was curious about my family.)*

In Home Eco. the girls were taught to sew by hand our graduation dresses which were all the same style and color white on white organza' with a red velvet sash. I received an award in Home Eco. It was a sterling silver medal with my name engraved on the back, but has the *name Mom registered me with when I first started school, "Frieda".* I found out when I graduated elementary school she had a best friend and gave me her name when I started kindergarten. *I didn't have the courage to tell my mother that I wanted my grandmother's Sicilian birth name Vitina, until I had to quit school to take care of my baby brother.* I felt I was old enough to have a say of what I wanted to be called.

I didn't attend my graduation because I came down with Strep throat. The cure was silver nitrate swab for the throat and hope for the best. It really helped and I had the summer to recuperate.

My First Kiss Summer 1933

I was eleven when I was first kissed by a boy who lived in one of the apartments in my maternal grandmother Anna's house. How dare this boy kiss me! I was in the hallway while going to my grandmother's apartment and it took me by surprise. The first thing I could think of was to slap his face and run. Every time I went to her house I was afraid to go into the hallway alone. Later I told my mother and Grandma Anna said that he liked me and his name was Jim. The problem was I didn't like him and was glad when he moved away.

My Brother Joe Was Born October, 1 1933

Finally my father and grandfather were happy, now a male child was born to carry on the Corso name. This meant to me, more responsibility. At this point I didn't mind, my sisters helped with taking care of him also. When he was two years he developed Polio and was taken to the hospital. This was when there was an epidemic and no cure for Polio. This was the first time when I saw my father and grandpa Corso cry when they saw my brother in the hospital.

Many children died and many were left crippled. My brother was one of the lucky ones he came out of it with no sign of the disease. When he came home, what actually did happen to him was that he was spoiled by everyone in the family. When he grew up, he joined the Air Force during the Korean Conflict.

Fortunately Dr. Salk found a cure and today there has not been any sign of this disease, for now. Every child is now inoculated.

High School Fall of 1938

In the fall a new high school was built on my father's route where he delivered mail. He knew most of the people at the school and asked if I could be enrolled, so I went to Franklin K Lane. The high school wasn't in our district but they made it a special favor for my father.

I guess he wanted to know that I would be safe and also he could keep an eye on me. Many times I would see him walking his route.

I remember the long walk to reach the school. It was over a mile one way about twenty two city blocks and there were no busses that went that route. In the spring, it was great but come winter coming home in the snow with no boots was when my feet would freeze. The bad part was my last period of the day I had swimming and most of the time my hair was wet.

My First Date, a Calamity 1938

My first real date was when I was fourteen. I was in high school and my life was changing, I thought I was grown up enough to have someone interested in me. It was the boy who delivered bread to our country store with his father. The storekeeper, Mr. Leo knew me since I was born. He also kind of knew that Frank was sweet on me. In those days girls had to be shy and demure, but Mr. Leo felt he had to play matchmaker. One morning, Frank asked me out on a date to see a movie. Naturally it had to be in the afternoon, why, because girls never went out at night unless they had a sister or friend with them.

Well, we went out quite a few times. Most of the time he made me feel that he owned me. This was the beginning of the conflict. He was jealous if another person talked to me and he never wanted to go out with another couple. There were times when my sister wanted to come with us but he refused to have her come. He also told me that I could not go out with my friends. I knew that this relationship was in trouble but I really liked him and wanted to try again and maybe he would change. On one of our dates we went to the movies and he was kissing me when he started groping, I felt uncomfortable and told him to stop.

Well I didn't tell anyone about the date and I told my mother I was going to the movies with my friend. As faith would have it one of my mother's friends was in the same movie theater and seen Frank kiss me.

When I came home my mother was waiting for me, she asked me about the movies and what the neighbor saw. I really didn't know what she said, but I told my mother nothing happened it was only a kiss. There was a big to do and I was forbidden to go out with any one unless they came and picked me up at the house.

I agreed with her and I really understood that. In a way I was glad she set the rules. When I told Frank that next time he wanted to go out he would have to pick me up at my house.

He wasn't pleased to do that. This meant that we tested the solution, it wasn't going to work. I promised my mother I would break off with him and it was the end of my first romance.

More Changes 1938

At this time of my life I had gone through many social changes and more to come. Being born at the time when radio was first invented, I remember this little box that my father had brought home. I was amazed at the programs that came out of it. Fibber McGee and Molly, this one was the definition of the soaps of today, but without the sex. Amos and Andy was a program of black America it was sort of a comedy and it was funny. Some families that could afford it had radios that looked like a piece of furniture; we had a table top one. Coming home from school the first thing I would do was to turn on the radio to listen to my favorite soap. My mother would shut it off because I had to do my homework first.

This doesn't happen in today's world.

September 1938

High school to me was freedom, a chance to learn what goals I wanted to pursue. My goal in high school was to become a dietitian. My dream was to visit and learn about many countries and their cuisine. It was because of the influence of what my grandmother taught me, and the cuisine of Italy and Sicily which are different. *I never believed that in my life* time *that I would travel and see where my family came from and many other countries.*

Chapter Five

Summer House

1939

I was fourteen when my father bought four acres of land in a sleepy town in upstate New York. Dad loved to hunt and wanted a cabin to stay at during hunting seasons. Mom also agreed it would be great to have a place in the summer, so we could get away from the hot city.

When he first took us up, we camped out. In those days, camping out was equivalent to being a pioneer. The "boys" as mom called Dad and my brother Joe cleared a small part of land and the first structure that went up was called the "back house". *Today's version called a "Port-a Potty."*

(The outhouse)

This back house in years to come turned in to a garden shed after we filled it up with dirt.

The boys worked hard to cut down the trees, clean up the brush, so that they could start to build the cabin. Cooking was my job on an open fire, no Gas Grill in those days. Down the road was a small spring, this was where we would get our water, the water was pure in those days.

An old fashion milk can was where we kept our water supply. To this day I have the original can we used. It is now painted white with painted flowers on it.

(Old Fashioned Milk Can)

Sleeping was another adventure. We all slept in little tents, not very comfortable and kind of scary, but we didn't know any better. We were pioneers and would survive. It took many weekends and vacations to get a nine by twelve structure built. This was the start of my parent's summer home and the first room built upstate.

On our many walks through the woods my brothers and I came upon a little road, it wasn't any ordinary road. At age fourteen these walks became exploration and adventure. We would try to name the trees, wild flowers, small animals, rabbits, squirrels and birds of all species. Sometimes if we were very quiet, we would come across deer grazing in the field at the end of this extraordinary road was a little brick house which I had seen for the first time I walked down the road at fourteen years old. Most of all I recall the trees that covered the road like a canopy with the changing seasons. After the spring rain, the air had the fragrance of rare perfume. The summers would turn a deep green and cool us from the sun. In winter, the canopy was brilliant with white snow that sparkled like crystal in the sun light. My favorite time was the fall with its golden colors and the sun dancing through crisp leaves. How beautiful nature was to expose me to the four seasons and always at the end of the road the house nested in the giant pines. My Dream House which someday I wanted to own.

As the years went by, we enjoyed the one room cabin although dad had added another room to the cabin. My brothers and sister and I slept on mattresses on the floor in the attic, where it was cozy and warm. Mom and dad slept downstairs.

(Our First Summer House)

My Education Ended

Early Part of March 1940

At age sixteen, I remember as if it was yesterday all the things life handed out to me in that year. My high school days were numbered, due to no fault of my own.

Mom had a best friend who lived next door, named Catherine she told me that my mother was pregnant and wanted to have an abortion. That made me feel guilty so I told my mother that the high school didn't have the classes that I needed to become a dietitian. As much as I hated to leave school I knew that she needed my help. Eight months later my brother Frank Paul was born on Ground Hog's Day February 2 1940. When he was three weeks old I became his mother. Mom went back to work and he was my baby to nurture, feed, bath and change his diapers, but most of all to love him the rest of my life. This lasted about a year and a half, when my Mom decided to send me out to work. At this time my sister Anna had to quit school to take care of my brother. My sister found that she couldn't handle taking care of him so Mom sent her to work with the telephone company and Mom stood home.

Growing up I was the son that my Dad had wanted. He would take me deep sea fishing. I remember the first time I went I got sea sick. After I got my sea legs I'll never forget the thrill of catching my first fish, a Sea Robin, it's such an ugly fish. Things went better when we went out after that. He introduced me to surf fishing, but that didn't go well I got the fish hook caught in my ear. I liked going out with the boat.

In the summer he taught me how to shoot a .22 rifle. He had a bale of hay in the back yard with a target on it. I was about sixteen when I first shot his pistol. He said, he was surprised that I held the gun with my two hands. In those days they only used one hand.

When Dad bought land upstate he asked me if I wanted to buy some land, I had fifty dollars in birthday money so I bought an acre of land near my father's. I felt very proud to have land that was all mine.

It was about that time my mother found out that Dad was having an affair with a woman he knew before he got married. She had lived on his postal route. When he would go hunting he would met her at the bungalow.

How Mom found out about his affair, her best friend whose husband went hunting with Dad told his wife and she told mom. I'll never forget this time in my life I was seventeen and as much as I loved my father I hated him for hurting my mother. How could he do such a thing? They had just had my baby brother and I had to leave school to take care of him.

My reasoning was if he wanted to leave my mother it was OK with me because I would be there for mom. She could stay home and I would go to work.

His excuse for the affair was he wanted this woman to get me a job in her office. My answer to him was I wouldn't work with this woman if I was starving. My Dad whom was my buddy who taught me so many things I said, we didn't need him, my sister and I would help our mother.

There was reconciliation and dad left the woman. They talked and mom said, she would stay home and I would go to work. The affair was over but my feeling about my father changed. He no longer was the person I could count on.

Latter Part of 1940

My mother's sister, Aunt Josie took me under her wing; this was the beginning of my career in the garment industry, I took to it like a duck takes to water. After all sewing my dolls cloths was an experience that came natural to me. With my first pay check in hand I had to give my mother half of it and the rest was mine. My sister and I slept together in an iron bed and I had always wanted a bedroom set. So I went to the furniture store in our neighborhood and bought a Rock Maple Bedroom set. The man who owned the store said I could pay him five dollars a week. That was fine with me, I still had one dollar for myself. In those days a dollar went along way. The set was fifty nine dollars and my credit was established. *Years later I bought furniture for my apartment from the same store.*

I didn't mind working with my aunt Josie in the garment industry, we were making women's skirts. This didn't last very long because I found that she made me do the zippers and belts, she did the straight seams. This was about the time when the war broke out in Europe, and I was offered a job making uniforms. I didn't take the job making uniforms because it was further away from home. She understood and I went to work on my own in a blouse factory. This boss taught me all the special machines and I worked there for quite a while. My father disapproved but it was time that I knew what I wanted to do.

Chapter Six

The Gulino Family

1941

This was the time that I first met Jim, my future husband. In writing about Jim I first must tell you of his family.

My father in law's name was Anthony Gulino. He was born in 1886 in the southern end of Sicily. Sciacca, the place where he was born is situated between Selinunte and Agrigento on the island. It is one of the oldest towns on the island and is renowned for hydro mineral resources, natural vapors and sweat grottoes. Founded in the 7th century BC and made into a health resort for people around the world.

Papa Gulino had an older brother from his father's first wife who had passed away; his name was James, and the name given to my husband when he was born.

Papa Gulino married Mama Gulino in 1911; Mama Angela Gulino was born in Sicily in 1894 and had passed away from a heart condition in 1932. She was only thirty eight and left five children. The family was devastated when their mother passed away.

Jim was close in age to his younger sister Jean, he was only twelve and she was seven. He had two older brothers Sal and Vincent and older sister Katie who were responsible for them when their father went to work. Sal and Katie were keeping company with their significant others.

My husband went to East New York Aviation School but left at sixteen to work as a baker's helper so he could help the family. He didn't stay there too long when a friend of his signed up for the Civilian Conservation Corps and so did Jim. He was at a camp in Emida, Idaho; his assignment was in forestry which consisted of cutting down burnt snags, making roads and signs. He served his six months and enjoyed every day of it. He left to come home for a job that was offered in a Stapling Company.

(Jim at the Civilian Conservation Corps.)

Certificate of Discharge

from

Civilian Conservation Corps

TO ALL WHOM IT MAY CONCERN:

THIS IS TO CERTIFY THAT * ___JAMES GULINO   OO2-268441___, A MEMBER OF THE

CIVILIAN CONSERVATION CORPS, WHO WAS ENROLLED ___January 12th, 1938___ AT
_(Date)

Camp S-125, Slaterville Springs, N.Y. IS HEREBY HONORABLY DISCHARGED THEREFROM, BY REASON

OF ** ___ETS - Declined to re-enroll.___

SAID ___JAMES GULINO___ WAS BORN IN ___Brooklyn___,

IN THE STATE OF ___New York___ WHEN ENROLLED HE WAS ___Seventeen___ YEARS

OF AGE AND BY OCCUPATION A ___Baker's Helper___ HE HAD ___Brown___ EYES,

___Dark___ HAIR, ___Fair___ COMPLEXION, AND WAS ___Five___ FEET

___Eight and a Half___ INCHES IN HEIGHT. HIS COLOR WAS ___White___

GIVEN UNDER MY HAND AT ___Camp Dix, N. J.___, THIS ___Thirtieth___ DAY

OF ___June___, ONE THOUSAND NINE HUNDRED AND ___Thirty Eight___

_____
(Name)
I. E. Corby, Capt. FA-Res.
(Title)

C. C. C. Form No. 2
April 5, 1938

*Insert name, as "John J. Doe".
**Give reason for discharge.

S-16171

Papa Gulino

His father was working for Nabisco Company in New York City. He would leave at four 'o clock in the morning to open up the Plant. He also would go on advertising jaunts with the Nabisco Band, He played the drums. When I first meet his father he made me feel that I belonged to the family. He invited me to eat supper with them and didn't want me to say no. He enjoyed speaking to me in our Sicilian language and I would answer his questions in the same way. Jim didn't speak Sicilian but understood every word we spoke.

His father never remarried. He said, he was too busy bringing up his family. Most of the children never gave him any trouble but except one, the middle one Vincent, who worked in a paper box factory but sometimes would get drunk and ride the subways. His older brother Sal would go after him and bring him home. Sal became the father figure of the family and when he married he still worried about the family. Before Jim and I got married he took me to see his brother and his wife Sadie before I met his father. Jim was always at his brother house when he needed advice. Sal and Sadie became my extended family.

How I Met My Husband Jim 1941

His sister Jean worked at the same shop, as a floor girl. (a person that finishes a garment for shipping). Her brother would meet her when we came home from work on the trolley car.

The young people of today only know the San Francisco Trolley.

I didn't realize that he was meeting her so that he could see me. He kept telling his sister that he wanted to go out with me. Well he finally asked me and I said, I couldn't. I was afraid that if I asked him to pick me up at my house he would say no.

Well, this went on till the summer of 1941. After asking me three times I told him he had to pick me up at my house if he wanted to go out with me. He said, YES. I will always remember the first time we went out. It was to our local movie theater, but the weather was a problem. We got caught up in a shower. We dodged the rain drops by going underneath the canopies of the stores along the way to the movies. After the movies we went to the ice cream parlor. Jim's favorite was a Pineapple Sundae. I had a Banana Split. We then went looking at the store windows, and expressed what we liked to have. I felt that I had known him for a long time. It was easy talking to him. We talked about what we wanted do with our lives, our families, and of course about World War II which had not started in America yet.

My First Trip to New York

Late Summer of 1941

I had told Jim that I had never been to NYC to see the Big Bands. He said he would take me on Saturday. When I told my father he said I could go but had to be home by 11 PM. Well, from my house to New York would take about an hour and a half, we had to take the Subway to get there in those days. We left about six so we could see the last show. I think that my father knew that we would never make it back at that time.

Von Monroe my favorite band leader was at the Paramount, feeling so happy to see such a person was like a dream come true. I still listen to his music. My favorite song was "My Devotion".

This is a part I really hate to write about because when Jim took me home my father was waiting for me, he was angry because we got home at 12:30.

He didn't make a scene but the next day he didn't want to listen to why we came back at that time. The next day I answered him that it was the first time to New York City and I didn't know how long it took to get home. His answer was I could not go back to New York again. Being eighteen and feeling that he didn't understand my explanation I defied him and told him that I would go again with Jim. *Maybe today it would be called child abuse but in those days taking a beating was the only way to punish a person. I was stubborn and didn't care.* At this point my mother intervened and told my father enough, and he stopped hitting me. I loved my father growing up but I guess I grew up that day and my father lost his daughter.

Not knowing why my father didn't want me to go out with Jim, he had someone else he wanted me to go out with. He was using the Sicilian culture of picking a husband for me.

When he calmed down he told me that it was a person who had just become a lawyer and had passed his Bar Exam. I told him that I liked Jim and he was the person I wanted to marry. Well this really infuriated him and said that I couldn't get married until I was 21. That was fine with me. The next words from my father was if Jim was 4f (this would have meant that he was unfit for military service) I would have to leave him. After all my father's investigations into Jim's life and family he accepted that this was it and he couldn't change my mind.

Chapter Seven

When My Beloved Grandmother Passed

July 1942

It was about two o clock in the morning; the door bell rang at our house. My father who was a sound sleeper didn't hear it. I was startled by the sound so I jumped out of bed, looked out of the front window and saw my father's sister Mary at the door. What was she doing here at that hour? I was so sure it was bad news.

By this time my father had awaken and came to open the door. She tried to whisper that something happened to my grandmother. This woman who was the light of my life, who gave me a philosophy of my life, which I still hold dear, how could anything happen to her? She had an inner strength which she gave freely to me and anyone that needed it. My father hurried and dressed and at this point so was I, he asked me where I was going and I said to grandmothers'. He didn't object for he knew I was always concerned and would be there when I was free.

Mama Vitina had a stroke and was on a cot in the dining room where we would all gather so many times. The stroke paralyzed her left side but her eyes still knew that we were there for her. They took her to the hospital where the doctors said she was critical. I remember my Aunt Gertie who was pregnant with her first child sitting outside in the car and refusing to go home until she heard that her mother passed away. I stood with her and we knew that our lives would never be the same without her.

She really needed her mother more than I did. She was the last child to get married and was close to her mother. I of course was close to my aunt, we were like sisters. There were things that Aunt Gertie didn't know about me and Grandmother, there were things she told me of her wishes when she passed away. There were some things I really didn't want to know. She has taken me to her trunk that she came over to this country with. In the trunk she showed me the clothes she wanted to tell my aunt that were to be used when she died. I remember telling my aunt of the little things we would do together, like fluffing up her feather bed. The mattress was made of duck feathers, which she made of the feathers grandpa and my father would go duck hunting with. Mama Vitina would take one end and I would take the other end and shank them up and down.

There were times that she would ask me if I would go to "City Line"? City Line was referred to as a stretch of stores about twenty blocks away which are between the boroughs of Brooklyn and Queens and in those days you would walk that distance. Nowadays one would drive instead. Most of the time she wanted me to pick up a jar of Ponds Cold Cream at the 5 & 10 cents store called Woolworth. She had the most beautiful skin and hair and eyes that changed color with what she wore.

(Grandma ViTina)

There was one thing that I really didn't want to know about "The Trunk" that came over from her country to this country. We went up to her bedroom and in one corner of the room there was this beautiful wooden round top trunk. At one time it held most of her treasures from the old country but as she opened it and showed me the clothes that she wanted my aunts to use when she died I wondered why she had picked me with this secret. She said, I was her name sake and knew that I would tell my Aunt Gertie of her wishes. She also said that the trunk was mine to keep. I promised her that I would keep her secret. I, of course needed her when I wasn't sure about a problem and when I needed her approval. When I first met my husband, I would tell her about Jim and how he would treat me and all the fun we had together. She was the one that said, he sounded like a good person and would make a good husband. Mama Vitina Passed away on July 19 1942, and as all these years that have gone by and until today she made me the person that I am.

Jim Was Drafted into the Army

October 1942

As life would have it Jim was drafted into the Army. I remember early in the morning of October 1942 when he left on a bus on his way to Oregon. He was stationed in Camp Adair and was in the Timber Wolf Division.

We wrote to each other and realized how much we had missed the times together, memories of how we took long walks in Highland Park; went bicycle riding, movies and of course the first time we went to see the Big Bands in New York City.

Much to my father's disappointment we got engaged on his next furlough, this was before Jim left for overseas. Before he left Jim called and asked me to meet him at the Paramount in Times Square, he had a big secret. Some of his buddies had gone AWOL from Fort Dix and so did Jim. We met the rest of them and that was the BIG SECRET. They were leaving for overseas the next day. I found out later that they weren't the only division that would go AWOL. When they arrived in France in 1943 the war was in full action.

This Map is of the lands through which the American soldiers and our Allies fighting their way to Berlin in World War II 1944.

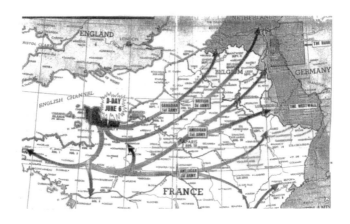

(Map of World War II Route of first Army)

After France the Timberwolf Division went to Holland, then down the Rhine River to Colognes.

At that time Jim was the scout of his outfit and would go and reconnaissance the area before the troops would go in. In December of 1944 in a little town in Germany Jim developed Pneumonia, and a case of acute Asthma and his wheezing could have given away their position he went back to the rear line and reported where the enemy was. He then was sent to a hospital in England in January 1945. After being in the hospital for about a month, he was then transferred to a hospital stateside in March 1945 at Fort DuPont, Delaware. He stayed at this place until the beginning of April then was sent on furlough for a month.

Our Wedding the Beginning of Our Life Together 1945

The Army had made it possible for us to get married. This was the year that I reached my 21st birthday so I remembered that I promised my father I would wait until then to get married. On April, 8 1945 we were married against my father's wishes, he thought it never would happened. What he didn't know was that we had saved our money so that we could get married. We knew what he would have said, he would say, he had no money for us.

We paid for our own wedding it was in a back room of a Bar named Anderson's. Of course my parents could not afford to give us a big wedding. Jim and I had a football wedding. *I believe you need an explanation of a football wedding, well; it's mostly what a small Italian wedding consists of, trays of sandwiches, salads, soda, beer and wine. We had trays of Italian cookies, Cream puffs, and Confetti's.* I don't remember too much about the wedding except that Jim came back and we were together again. We had a small band that played Italian music. Our gifts were money, small donations of five & ten dollar bills. My Godmother Aunt Mary held the bag of money and she counted it out to four hundred dollars, in those times it was a lot of money which we saved.

On our honeymoon I wrote my mother a postcard expressing my feeling of how I felt, "Life can be Beautiful". She thought I was kinda Crazy! About two days into our honeymoon at The Hotel New Yorker I received a telephone call from my mother and she told me that my father wouldn't eat and he was sick. Every time my father was under stress his ulcer acted up.

Jim and I took the train from New York City to Queens to see my father. He was in bed and really did look sick. Mom had made some chicken soup and when we got there I fed him some. He was happy to see me and asked when we were coming home. We told him that we were going to Atlantic City at the Hotel Dennis after our stay at the hotel New Yorker. Jim and I spent the rest of the day with them and then went back to the hotel. Dad realized that we were very happy and that maybe he was wrong about my marrying Jim.

The Army had sent us on R&R *Rest and Recuperation* and we considered it our Honeymoon. One week at the Hotel New Yorker and two weeks at the Hotel Dennis in Atlantic City, *this is now the Baily.*

It was the happiest days of our lives. While we were on our honeymoon in Atlantic City we heard that the War had ended. It seemed that at first we didn't believe it, but our friends at the Hotel called to tell us it was true and we made a date so we could celebrate the news.

After Our Honeymoon 1945 Summer

Jim returned to *active duty* and was stationed in Rome NY State as a guard to watch the German prisoners. They worked on a farm picking peas, Jim said, not any one of them ever thought of escaping. They realized that they were treated fairly and that they were safe. When most of the prisoners talked with Jim they said, when the time came to be sent back to their country most never wanted to go back.

Jim was there from July to October when he was sent to Rowe's Hospital in Utica N Y, because he had another bout of pneumonia and Asthma.

After being away from each other for almost six months; Jim called everyday and wished that he was with me. The days went by and I realized how much I needed Jim and my mother. Now, the shoe was on the other foot, I needed her support. Jim was still in the Army and I still lived at home. Mom was happy to have me there but she realized that maybe we needed a place of our own. She said, we could have the downstairs apartment and she would take the upstairs one. Jim agreed because when he came home on furlough we would have our own apartment.

I remember Mom and me planning how to fix the apartment. There were four rooms: living room, dining room, kitchen and bedroom. Of course my idea of what kind of furniture that I liked was different than my mothers. We went to the local stores in City Line that were in Brooklyn, where most of the stores were. They were owned by individual people, which now would be called *mom & pop stores*. In the store with Mom it only took one hour to pick out the furniture. What Mom didn't know was I had already had picked out what I wanted before stopping at the store on my way from work. My Mother was upset that I spent one thousand dollars. She didn't realize that we had saved our wedding money and Jim would send me money and I was working, I reassured her that I had the money to pay for what I bought. When I told Jim about what I picked out he also was worried about the money, but I told him that I had saved all the money from the wedding and the money he was sending home.

Our first bedroom set was Blond solid Oak; the living room furniture was a blue print sofa and two arm chairs. The best piece that I really loved was the fake fireplace this was always a part of a dream that would complete my home.

In October of 1945 we soon found out he was released from the army from Rhoads General Hospital and that he wanted to get a job. He applied for a job in the Post Office as a postman, he also took the Federal test and passed it, but as time went on and the winter months came Jim came down with pneumonia. He worked for about a year and half when the doctor told him to get a job inside so that he would not be exposed to the winter weather.

Pregnant 1946

I was still working in a blouse factory on Atlantic Avenue, for Italian bosses, when I realized that I was pregnant. When one of my bosses found out they asked me to leave. *This would never happen in this day and age.* Anyway it was in my favor, so now I could enjoy making plans for my own baby. What I most enjoyed was that mom was not working and we were making plans to redo the apartment and make room for the baby. We knew that we had to get Dad's permission. That was because he would do the work. He would have to build a partition and put in another door to the bathroom. To our surprise he agreed. *According the old custom when he built the house the bathroom was to be in the hall.* Dad really wanted to redo the apartment and he also put in new kitchen cabinets. He did the work with a little help from Jim. Jim knew how to use tools since he had built an airplane wing in New York Aviation Vocational School. His father couldn't keep it because they lived in apartment. Jim said he learned a lot helping my Dad.

With all the construction that was going on it was almost Christmas and time that my baby was due. I thought that maybe I would give birth for the holiday. To take my mind off worrying about when the baby was due Mom took me shopping to Jewish town. They had pushcarts and fresh foods and were only open until before sundown on Friday, the start of Saturday their Holy Day. The only problem shopping there was we had to take the train home with lots of heavy bags. This was the one time that heavy bags really mattered. When we returned home my labor pains started, I called Dr. Iorio and he said I had time and that he would pick me up at five thirty in the morning. *In those days the doctors were your personal friend and had more time with their patients.*

My First Born 1947

My first born, Angela came into the world as a breech baby. I was in labor for 16 hours. All I can remember was the nurses kept telling me to walk. Of course I didn't know what was going on. Why was I told to keep walking? Mac was the name of my nurse and when I finally asked her what was wrong, her answer was they were waiting for the doctor to come in. *At the time as far as I was concerned he was coming in from China.* Actually, I later found out that they were waiting for my baby to turn in my womb. Well, she never did, and a C section was the last thing the doctor would do at that time. *Today you can pick the time and day you want to have your baby.* Doctor Ioiro was an old doctor and the best O.B. of that time. When the baby didn't turn he knew what he had to do. They put me out and before I went out went out I felt the doctors fingers inside the birth canal and he turn the baby by the feet and that was all I remembered, until I saw her later. How happy to see her when they brought her to me.

She was 6lb 12 0z. with red marks on her face. I took the blanket off to see if she was perfect, my own baby. After having taking care of my baby brother for six years I must admit that taking care of her was going to be easy. This was one of the happiest times of my life. Jim was home from the war and we had a daughter.

She would be the child that I could dress and nurturer and dream of what she was going to be when she grew up.

My brother was six and he also was happy, he had someone he could be with. *The rest of his life he was the big brother that my daughter had.*

Job in Nabisco 1947

At this time Jim's father said that there was an opening at his place in New York for a job. His father worked at Nabisco most of his life and was in charge of opening the building. He also was in charge of the workers and any problems that came up during the day. In the early days he would travel with the Nabisco Band, and played the drums. They traveled thru the West and sometimes played in the Buffalo Bills Show. *We still have one of his drums.* Jim's father said that that job was working nights and watching the sugar wafers come off the ovens. The heat from the ovens helped his condition. Jim accepted the job and didn't mind working nights; he was a night person any way. We were starting to get settled with our lives and very happy that things were going as planned. Our bills were paid and Jim took advantage of the G I Bill. *G I Bill was for veterans that* came home from the war and could go back to school and start a new career. Jim took Professional Photography, and it was one of his hobbies before he went into the Army. He went to school during the day and worked at night. He graduated with seven hundred ninety hours as a Professional Photographer.

After graduation he decided to take his hobby to a new level, taking weddings, portraits, baby pictures and Christmas cards for families. His weekends were always busy working in his dark room in the basement of my Mom's house. Most of the money he made we saved for maybe a house of our own.

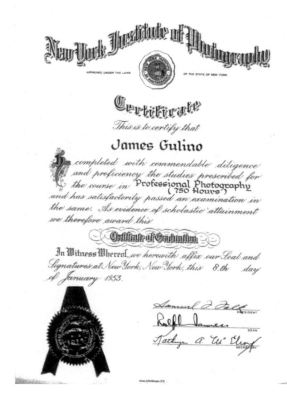

Chapter Eight

Mom Took Charge of Her Life

1948

This was the year Mom and Dad decided to move upstate. Dad had put two more rooms to the house up in Palenville. Much to my mother's feelings about moving, she didn't want to go up there in the winter. Of course my father got his way. Most of the women in those days never had any say. They kept the basement apartment and rented the top floor of the city house.

We of course were still living at the house so they knew that we would take care of the house, and the tenant. I would collect the rent and send it to them. Mom hated the winter's upstate. She said all winter she WOULD just see rabbit tracks. She told my father that she wanted to go to Florida in the winter. Dad's answer was she would get used to the winter.

My baby brother was going to school up there and my father assumed that mom had to stay upstate. Well as soon as my brother had summer break from school my mother decided that she would go to Florida with my brother without my father. This came as shock to my father; he came down to the city to tell me what my mother did. Well, he didn't get any sympathy from me and I told him that he should close the house and go down to Florida. Of course he had no alternative, he could not live without her.

(Mom and Dad in Florida)

My Life Was Changing 1950-1955

I Gave birth to my daughter Nancy on September 19 1950. She was named after my mother. After she was born I didn't understand what was wrong with me at the time. I realized later on that I had postpartum depression. It wasn't a time in my life that I want to remember. There was so much to be thankful for and yet there was something missing.

At first I thought something was wrong in my head, every time I went out of the house I would have an anxiety attack. It felt like my body and mind didn't belong to me.

Maybe it was mental, missing my mother who was living upstate and was with me when I gave birth to my first child, but now I was alone. It was time to see my doctor he told me I was fine only I was a little anemic so every week I went for injections of iron and B12 shots.

My mother came down from upstate to see me and gave me a talking to, she said, that she would put my girls in a home if I didn't take control of myself. That really scared me. Time went on and the iron and B 12 shots helped. It took about a year and half before I felt like myself again. In 1953 I decided to go back to work again. My Aunt Anna lived a few blocks away and took my Nancy to stay with her. Angela was in school and would walk to her house after school. After work I would pick them up and head home, and get ready for the next day. Things were getting back to normal.

In Italian Families, Boys Come First 1955-1956

The older of my two brothers, Joe was in the Air Force for six years and when he came home from the Korean Conflict he took my mother's apartment in the basement. I thought that he would take care of himself but that didn't happen. He was my other child to take care of. Joe was spoiled; he was the first boy among his three sisters. Also because he had Polio we all treated him special, my father had the son to carry the Corso name. In the Italian culture the first son is always treated with respect. Most of the time I had to make special food for him, because he didn't like pasta, and take his clothes to the cleaners, and most of the time pay the bill. This went on for some time until my husband said enough already. This was when I told my brother that we couldn't afford it any more. I thought that if my brother had a girlfriend maybe he would have someone to take care of him.

This person that I was working with had a sister that had come to visit her from Germany. She wanted her sister to stay in America so we decided to introduce them to each other. The match worked! What happened after this was something that till today I'll never forget, my brother wanted my apartment and asked my father to tell me that I should move because my brother was getting married and didn't like living in the basement. In the Italian Tradition the first son can ask for anything he wants because he carries the family name.

My mother was against that decision but again my father won. She felt my brother couldn't take care of the responsibility of the tenant, when they were down South. I think my father realized that when he asked Jim to use his G. I. Bill to pay his mortgage and Jim said no he wanted to keep the option for our house.

Now We Were On Our Own 1957

After eleven years of living in the house where I was born and where my children were born, this altercation came as a surprise. I loved my brother but I felt hurt that he would have my father make this decision. Jim and I had often thought about buying our own house so maybe this was the time to do it. We had saved money that Jim made with his hobby of taking weddings and portraits so it would be enough for a down payment. The girls were in school and Jim and I were working so we felt that we could make it.

House in Woodhaven 1958

We bought our house in Woodhaven. It was a brick two family house with a three room apartment on the second floor and a finished basement. When we saw the house it was the only brick house in the style of an English Tudor and it was in excellent condition. We bought the house and moved in October of 1958.

This was about the time that the Nabisco plant was moved to Fairlawn New Jersey. We were asked if we would go to Fairlawn but we decided that we could make a go of it. I was working in the garment industry and Jim was offered a job in Continual Baking Company, it was night work but it made it easy so Jim would be home when the girls came home from school. There were times when Jim had to go in early and the girls were considered Latch Key Kids. In those days it was safe for them to come home alone. *I can't imagine them doing that in this day and age.*

(House in Woodhaven)

We rented the apartment to a school Nurse, Ruth who became part of our family and was also home when my children came home from school. She was with us for seventeen years until she retired to take care of her mother in Pennsylvania; *we kept in touch for a number of years.*

When my father first saw the house he was surprised that we had bought such a good house. Jim's father thought the house looked like a little church. It had a door with a stain glass window. He loved what we had bought, such a beautiful house, he said. We had many family parties and holidays in our finished basement where most of our families came together.

The Year I Got My Drivers License 1959

Living in Woodhaven was wonderful but without a car made life a little hectic. It was a must to get my license. Shopping, taking the girls to the doctor was taking its toll and there wasn't enough time in the day to take buses. I felt that I could spend more time with the girls if I had a car. I decided that it was time to learn how to drive. This was going to be a tricky problem if I asked Jim, he would say, it wasn't necessary and walking was good for your health. I really wanted to drive and found out how to do it. A person I worked with told me about this person who taught men how to become bus drivers for the city. Well, I met Casey and he would pick me up after work and I would drive for an hour. It only took three lessons and Casey said I could use his car for my driving test. I passed the test, but what happened next was, Jim found out my little escapade when he got the mail. He called me at work and told me that I received a letter from the Department of Motor Vehicles. I told him to open the letter. He really wasn't angry, but wanted to know when I had the time to get my license. He was a little upset but after I told him he said he was glad I used the time doing something that I wanted. He was also glad he didn't have to get his license. He had learned to drive in the Army but never applied to getting his civilian license. I also told him that I wanted a new car. His answer was do you think we could afford it. My first car was an American Motors Classic, color Dusty Pink. *We had the car for thirteen years and I enjoyed it very day, we even used it for transporting big items, by taking the back seat out.*

Things Were Going Well 1960

Our family life was taking a pattern of routine, Jim was working nights. The girls were both going to the same school and they would come home and do their home-work. On one day a week we went to our church St. Elisabeth for piano lessons, the church was only a block away. My oldest daughter Angela was responsible for her sister Nancy. After lessons they would walk home together and not allowed out until I came home. Sometimes I would pick them up and Sister Bennosis would tell me that Angela was very talented but Nancy didn't like taking lessons. Nancy would tell me that the Sister would hit her fingers with the pointer. This presented a problem, I spoke to the Sister and asked her not to hit her fingers and that she was afraid of her. Ruth our tenant who was a school nurse was home at the same time the girls came home.

We were fortunate to have Ruth upstairs for seventeen years. She watched them grow up and was very fond of them. My daughters are two different people but love each other for whom they are. Even today they are always close to each other.

(Picture of the Girls)

Chapter Nine

One of the Worst times

1962–1963

Thru all the years Papa Gulino loved coming to our house. This time he needed care and asked if he could stay with us. Papa Gulino had a heart attack and the rest of the family could not accommodate him. During all the years I respected him and we took him in. We had the finished basement so we made it comfortable for him. He loved staying with us and sometimes would make supper for us. He was with us for three months and if it wasn't for his son Vincent who was living with him and came home from being in jail for vagrancy, he probably would have stayed with us forever.

The Christmas of 1963 was one that I would never forget. A few days before Christmas my sister in law Jean asked her father if he would like to have dinner for the holiday at her house. In all the years that she was married she never had any of the Gulino's over for any holidays.

Of course Papa said, he didn't want to go to her house. When he told me about it I gave my opinion and said he should go because after all maybe she realized that he wasn't well and he was getting older. This was the worst opinion I ever made. My father in law passed way on December 23 1963.

The irony was he really didn't want to go to her house and all of the family spent the holiday in the funeral parlor instead.

(Jim took this Photograph of his Father)

Big Decisions 1964

In 1964 this was the beginning of a period when Jim and I had to make some big decisions. Jim's older brother Vincent, who never married and lived with his father, was an alcoholic and would get drunk, ride the subway after work and sometimes didn't come home. Now, the question was who was going take responsibility for Vincent. The Gulino family had a meeting and none of the family wanted to take on the responsibility. This time I thought that we were going to have to take him in and I felt that Vincent had to realize that he had to take care of himself. I suggested that Jim and his oldest brother Sal would help Vincent stay in the apartment and they would come once a week and see what he needed. This was the only way it could work. There were times when I would go with Jim and I would take Vincent shopping. We were really surprised that Vincent really started to understand that he had to take care of himself.

I Took the Girls to Florida June of 1964

It came time when my family came first. Both of my daughters were graduating, Angela from high school and Nancy from eighth grade. As a graduation present I told Jim that I wanted to take the girls to Florida to see my parents and I needed some time after all that had happened that year. We went and the girls and my mother and father went to The Vizcaya, a beautiful Manson on Biscayan Bay in Miami Florida and Sea World also many of the other places but most of all the girls and I loved to go fishing on the pier. It reminded me of when my father took me fishing and crabbing when I was his buddy; Mom and Dad came back home in the spring of 1965.

Every year they would leave after Election Day and come back for Easter. We would all come upstate for the holiday and stay the week end. Most of the time we would have a reunion and most of the family were there and have Easter dinner at our parent's house. All our children and their cousins were there and happy to see each other and they would play games and enjoy themselves.

Chapter Ten

The Dream that Came True

Summer of 1965

Every time we went upstate Jim and I would walk down our favorite road. In the summer the trees would cover the road and it was cool and green. The winter season was the most beautiful of all. After we felt that we were walking through a canopy that changed color with each season.

One particular weekend, we came up to see my parents for the summer. Taking our usual walk Jim and I walked down our favorite road we were devastated to see my favorite house gutted by fire. The sign said "Keep Out." Nothing was left except the Brick walls. The Dream I had at fourteen was shattered. We asked ourselves so many questions which needed answers. How could we abandon my Dream? Could we save it? How much damaged did the fire cause? Who owned it?

Jim and I had always wanted a country home but when we saw the condition of the house, could we salvage it? There was a fireplace that was in working condition and this would come in handy when we would come up to work on the house. I also love to have a working fire place. Jim and I had to make a decision, could we tackle this tremendous job? Jim knew how I felt I about the house since I was fourteen and he also wanted to prove that he could turn it into something beautiful.

We hurried back to my Dad and asked if he could find out who owned the house, and that we were interested in buying it. Dad had a hard time finding the owner. He asked one of the neighbors and he told him that he was a retired policeman and lived alone and most of the time went to a bar every day. He also told Dad how the fire started. He wanted to light a cigarette on the gas stove and it blow up. He was very fortunate he survived the blast. It was said, that he was so drunk he didn't know what happened.

When Dad did find him at the bar he said the place was condemned. Dad asked how much he wanted for the place, one thousand seven hundred dollars. Dad had looked over the house and said it could be saved but it would be a big job. He said that the house was on solid rock. So he answered some of the questions; so Yes we purchased the house.

(The road leading to my dream house)

(Pictures of my dream house before we purchased it!)

How Could We Abandon My Dream October 1966

Winter was just around the corner and there were burnt holes in the roof. This was the first construction problem that had to be taken care of. Another problem was boarding up all the windows and we put in an old door that Dad had. We were lucky that Dad knew someone who would put a new roof on the house. We met Pete the roofer on the weekend and we described what type of a roof we wanted (Hip Roof). He was taking the old one off completely and taking all the old stuff away. We agreed on the price $ 1,700 and he would start immediately before the snow flies. The cost of the roof was as much as the price of the house.

Jim worked as a baker at the Continental Bakery in Jamaica Queens. He worked nights and I worked days. It wasn't the best routine but it served the purpose. I would pick him up at the plant about 1:00 AM and drive up to the country about 4:00 AM. When we arrived there was a back room we fixed that wasn't burnt and we had a place to sleep, and no squirrels could get in.

We would catch a few hours of sleep and then started to work on the house. Slowly we took out all the burnt beams and all the burnt furniture out, we went down to the bare walls. The only insulation in the house was the acorns in between the walls that the squirrels brought in. We took out five truck loads of burnt rubble. Pete put on a new roof so if it snowed the house was secured.

It was November and Mom and Dad left for Florida, so we went back to the city, but it was too cold up there to work on the house. It would have to wait until Spring to do any work.

Back in the city Jim and I started to make plans for the house. The floor plan which we agreed on was two bedrooms, a bathroom, living room, dining area, and kitchen which unfolded into each other. I wanted the rooms to be open so that we could see every one when we had company; it also made the house look bigger. Jim of course didn't think about the rooms, he was thinking about what kind of windows and doors to put in. He was busy doing research on plumbing and electric installation. The house had so many problems to solve and very little money, so Jim wanted to do the work himself. The winter passed and Spring was almost upon us.

Ray and Angela's Engagement 1966

At this time my daughter was seeing a young man named Ray, I didn't think at the time that this relationship was going anywhere. When I first met Ray I wondered about his relationship with my daughter. He was going out with someone else and when he had a problem with her he would come to our house and talk to Angela. They would sit on the stoop and talk for hours. I asked my daughter, why was he always at our house when he had a girlfriend. She said that he liked talking to her. I took it upon myself and called his mother and told her to talk to her son about his girlfriend. She did talk to her son and told him that he should marry my daughter Angela. It was about this time Ray joined the Army in 1965 and became a paratrooper with the 101st Airborne Division and then to Vietnam. Our Angela was working at AT&T and Ray was still in Vietnam, they wrote to each other and were engaged after he came home from Vietnam. Raymond who had just come back from Vietnam decided that they wanted to get married in August of 1967. This didn't come as a surprise.

Spring, a Very Expensive Year 1967

This was going to be an expensive and busy year. All winter Jim and I planned what we were going to do first at the house upstate. The roof was finished, we had to secure the rest of the house and take off all the boards, so the windows were our first priority.

We found a lumber yard in Saugerties that had a person who helped us with the windows. They had to be special ordered as well as the door. This was going to be the only thing we could do for this year on the house.

Angela and Ray's Wedding 1967

My daughter Angela wanted me to make her own wedding gown. I knew that as I was a seamstress and most of my life I made all our clothes and made all my dresses and some for special occasions, but this was going to be my first time at making a wedding gown.

We had a fabric store in our area where I bought my material from this man named Abe. He had become a friend and always knew what kind of material I needed. When I told him that my daughter was getting married and I wanted something special, he decided to import Chantilly Lace and slipper satin for the lining. Angela loved the material, so we bought what we needed. The style of the gown was very simple because the material was beautiful. We decided to put crystal beading on the gown for Good Luck.

Every Sunday morning after church we would sit on the bed and sewed beading on the gown. When we finished Angela's gown, I realized that I needed a gown for the wedding and went back for my material. He had a white and gold treaded Brocade. The bridesmaids bought their gowns in New York City. Things went as scheduled, we found a hall, had the date with our church, the boys rented their tuxedos, and we did a million other things to make sure that the wedding was perfect. Everything did go perfect but of course we could not count on the weather, it rained part of the day but that didn't make any difference. It was a beautiful wedding

They were married on August 26, went on their honeymoon upstate and they went to Connecticut where Ray was going to school. When Ray came home in 1967 from Vietnam and he took advantage of the G.I. Bill that made Veterans eligible for education. Ray had applied to the Culinary Institute of America at Yale in New Haven, Connecticut at that time.

(Ray and Angie's Wedding)

(Immediate Family)

Chapter Eleven

Another Big Problem

1969

Mom went to the hospital for an operation on her legs for varicose veins, her feet were bothering her and she couldn't walk. She had bad veins when she was young and having eleven pregnancies didn't help. She had six miscarries and five of us. At the time that she was there the doctors told my father that they wanted to take a few tests. They thought that she was confused and that something was wrong with her mind. Dad knew that she would forget things and couldn't cook any more. He sometimes had to dress her. He didn't tell us what he was going through. He confided with Jim what was happening with Mom. When Jim told me what Dad was doing, I told him it was about time he took care of Mom. Subconsciously, I really had this resentment that my father was this demanding person who always had his way with all of us. Jim said, he was very serious and he didn't want anyone to know. This went on for a few more years until the family knew Mom was in the advanced stages of Alzheimer's (Dementia) at that time.

Tina Maria Heyman 1970-1971

On May 12 1970 our first granddaughter was born, and my Angela had the same complication as I had when she was born. Angela also had hours before the baby was born; I guess it was in the genes. Everything turned out fine and the best surprise was when my daughter told me that they named the baby Tina Maria. I was so proud and honored to have her named after me. Baby Tina had blue eyes, and light hair and was perfectly normal. As time went on she developed allergies and the doctor suggested that they should move to the country.

My brother had built an A Frame house on land that my father gave him. It so happened that my brother had decided to buy a small farm in a small town in Chipley in the Pan Handle of Florida.

Ray and Angela loved the country and often were up at my parent's house for vacation. My Mother and Father loved their great granddaughter. My Dad would teach her how to plant in the vegetable garden. He also played games and made her laugh a lot. She had such a hardy laugh.

Ray and Angela made up their mind that they didn't want to live in the city and that they would buy my Brother Frank's house; in April of 1972 they bought it. After graduation Ray had an offer to Cook for a boy's school in upstate in Mill Brook, New York. They didn't move into the A Frame until 1974. Since then, they have lived there for thirty five years.

(Angie and Ray's House)

Too Many Needed Me 1972

I was still working in the garment industry and working in New York. I really didn't want to work so far from home but my boss Julie ask me to come there because most of the workers didn't want to go to New York. It meant that they had to take the subway and spend an hour on the train. At the time Jim wasn't feeling very good and I hated to leave him alone. We were going to the doctor and he said maybe if he would go to Arizona he would feel better. I took off from work in March and made plans to go to Tucson Arizona. We rented a three room Efficiency and took long walks and short trips to see the scenery. We took a Bus trip to the Grand Canyon and it made me feel how insignificant I was, standing on the rim of the vastness of the Canyon. I thought of all the people in the world and we were only an ant who had to survive in the world of today. I was only an ant. Who was I!?!.

Within the month that we were there Jim came down with a bad case of asthma and I had to take him to the V.A. hospital in Tucson. They said he was dehydrated and an i.v. in him, we were there all day. We had thought of buying a Condo out there but it seemed that he wasn't feeling any better regardless so we returned home to be with our family.

Now What's Next? 1973

Most of the time my parents went down to Miami Florida for the winter, they were (snow birds) people that left the northern part of the country for the warm climate of the southern states. They usually would go away after Election Day and come back for Easter. This went on for 20 years. They had friends that would meet them there and they became their extended family. The men would play cards or go fishing and the women would go shopping or spend the afternoon sitting on the veranda talking, knitting and discussing what to cook. There was a nursing home next door from where they were staying and Mom would spend time with the women that lived there. She once said that she would like to be placed there when she got old.

It was March of this year when they came home early from Florida. Mom and Dad had an anniversary coming up on April 23 1973 and Dad wanted to have a party and invite his and Mom's sisters and brothers to celebrate their 50th Year. He asked my sister Anna to help with the arrangements for the party. I was busy with making plans for my younger daughter Nancy's wedding on June 2 1973. I didn't have very much time for all arrangements of his party so my sister Anna helped him. Mom needed a gown and she wanted me to make it. Of course I went to my favorite material store and Abe had just the material for the gown, gold brocade. I had 2 weeks to make the dress, just in time for the party.

Everything went well with their anniversary party. They had most of brothers and sisters and the people that were in their bridle party. We all went to church and Mom and Dad renewed their wedding vows in the church that they were married at, St. Fortunate. It was such a beautiful day and we will never forget that day.

(Immediate Family)

It was the summer of 1973 when Dad became ill. He always planted his vegetable but this time he didn't have the strength to do it. He went to the hospital and they didn't know what was wrong. They packed him in ice to bring the fever down. When I arrived at the hospital saw him in a tub of ice I spoke to the doctor and told him he was going to get pneumonia, not knowing that he already had it. When the tests came back they found that he had Lung Cancer but we were told that his condition was inoperable. The doctors said that he may have a short time to live.

Not knowing how much time Dad had, we still had the plans of Nancy's wedding. It was too late to change the plans and I had a heavy heart and I knew that bad times were coming, Dad was happy that he was feeling better and that he would be at Nancy and Joe's wedding. I remember that I was sewing beads on Nancy's gown and wishing that everything would turn out well. Maybe Dad would have more time and see the rest of his great grandchildren.

(Mom and Dad renewed their vows on their 50th)

(Starting Left to Right: Jean, Anna, Me, Mom, Dad, Joe and Frank)

Nancy and Joe's Wedding 1973

Nancy's wedding was sort of sad for me; I felt that some phase of my life was ending. Maybe it was the empty nest syndrome and maybe my problems were only beginning, with my father's condition and what was going to happen with my mother.

I had asked Dad not to go down South for the winter. I told him that our neighbor had an empty apartment that they could stay up north so we could take care of him and mom.

His answer was "Come hell or high water he would go down." He did go down and this time they flew down, he always drove down. They were only there since November when at Christmas time one of his friends called me and told me that he was very sick and Mom could not take care of him. Mom's condition had progressed and she didn't know how to dress herself or much less than to cook something for Dad

My brother Joe and I took the plane down to Miami to see what was going on. We found Mom very confused and upset. Dad was in bed and could not do anything to help her. We decided that I would take them home to my house and take him to the Veterans Hospital in New York. My brother took care of Dad and I took care of Mom. We gathered all their personnel belonging's and left most of their things that they had accumulated over 20 years. We called the airlines to make plans to take them home. I explained the circumstance of my father's condition and that it was an emergency and that we had to bring him to the hospital in New York. They were very accommodating and we left the next day. His friend from the hotel took us to the airport. When we arrived home we called the hospital and they said to bring him in the morning. They took many more tests and the doctor said that his cancer was inoperable and a month later he passed away on February 9 1974. I knew that we had our differences but when he was going to die I realized how much I loved my Dad. He was only looking out for my future when I was young. Just to know that he confided in my husband about my mother's condition and told Jim not to tell me, I realized how much he loved me. Of course Jim told me what Dad said. Before Dad passed away he asked me to take care of Mom, and also how our lives would change.

(Nancy and Joe)

Nancy and Joe's Apartment 1974-1975

Nancy and Joe had an apartment in Joe's parent's house. I didn't have much time to spend with my daughter Nancy, who was a new bride and living in a new environment and really needed me. One night at 2:00 in the morning she called and told us that there was a mouse in the bedroom. Joe worked nights for the water company and wasn't home and she didn't know what to do. She lived in her mother in laws house and didn't want to bother her. Jim and I went to her apartment and calmed her down. Nancy was a happy child but now she was on her own and Jim and I worried about her.

That year my life took on so many problems. Coping with my mother's condition, Nancy needing me, and Angela in Connecticut having her baby... What do I do first?

Chapter Twelve

1974

My mother at that time was my first priority; she was completely confused and didn't even remember that my father had died. *Now What?*

The only happiest thing that happened in 1974, our first Grandson Thomas James Heyman was born on April 26. He was born in Sharon, Connecticut and I couldn't be there for my daughter Angela, I had my mother to worry about.

I was working in the garment industry so that meant I would have to stay home or go to work late. My boss was very considerate and told me no matter what time I would get to work he didn't mind, just come in.

I remembered my mother's two sisters whom were retired and would go to the senior center every day. Aunt Mary and Aunt Nashua offered to take her with them to the center. The mornings were very hectic; she didn't want to take her bath and didn't want to go with her sisters. It would take an hour to convince her to go, but she wanted to come home right away.

The center closed at 3:30 and I asked my sister Anna if she could take Mom until I came home at 5:00. She did it for a couple of days and told me it didn't fit into her schedule.

The situation with my job was not working out well, because the ride from Woodhaven to New York would take one hour by subway. I had to make another decision, leave my job and take one nearer to home. There was a little dress shop a few blocks away so it made it easier to cope with Mom.

My boss whom I had worked for 17 years understood my responsibility and wished me luck. My salary went down but that didn't matter because I felt I could manage Mom being nearer to home.

*There is an Old Italian saying. A mother can take care of all her children, but not one child can take care of one mother.

How True... As I looked at my Mother who had nurtured five children, and now I was incapable of taking care of her. The burden fell on me, my sisters and brothers were all in the same boat as me. Their families needed them. *What was next?* I left my job, took Mom in our house tried to make her happy and comfortable. All she wanted was just to be with me all day and night. She loved my husband but sometimes she would say... Who is he? What is he doing here? Other times when she was lucid she would say to Jim, Smile James. She always loved Jim and he loved her. She became the mother he didn't have.

She was now my child, who needed constant care. Our roles were reversed, I became her mother.

When she was diagnosed with what was called Dementia at that time in 1970, they didn't have a medical name for the disease. I wanted to know if there was any help that I didn't know about. I took her to a neurological doctor. The only thing he did was, ask her questions. She couldn't answer some simple ones, like what day was it? Who was the present president? What were the names of her children? At the end of twenty minutes he told me that she had Dementia and there was no cure for this decease, *which now is called Alzheimer's.* He pointed to a file cabinet and said he would be a rich man if he found a cure. Why wasn't there a cure? How many older people ended up with it and they were labeled crazy. How many young and older ones were put in institutions? I went home with my Mom with still a million questions and no answers until today and still NO cure.

How could I tell my Mother that she could never go back upstate to her home, and she never remembered that Dad had passed away?

There was a day that my sister Anna said, that she would like to take Mom for the weekend. I really didn't know if she wanted to go. Mom went, but what happened next we will never forget. Mom wondered from my sister's house and my sister called and we all ran to her house. We asked the neighbors if they had seen her and they said that she went up to the El train station. We all went up to the waiting room and she told us that she was going upstate to her house. The only way she would come down from the El station on Liberty Ave in Ozone Park, was that I promised her I would take her home on the weekend. Of course she couldn't be left alone up there.

As faith intervened, my oldest daughter and her husband Ray had just bought my brother Frank's A Frame house, which was across the meadow from my mother's house. Frank had bought a small farm in Chiply, Florida, and started a business growing steer for Veal. Angela who loved her grandmother had grown up with her until she was ten years old said that she would take care of her. We would try anything to make her happy. This went on for about a few months, Angela and Ray wanted her to eat with them but she didn't want to. Angela would go shopping with her and bought her food that she could eat without putting on the gas stove. Most of the time she would throw the food in the woods and say she had no food. Angela would make her a dish and she took it home to eat. There was another problem, she saw herself in the mirror and told us that an old lady was in her house and she was going to kill her. *This is typical of this disease, their mind goes back in time, when they were young or maybe when she took the train home when she was young.* She would speak in her native tongue. One day Angela went to see if she needed anything, she was not to be found. Someone said, she was walking down the road to the main road. She had a friend who lived in Palenville about a mile way and went there without telling my daughter. Angela called her friend and told her she was there and went to pick her up.

Now, it was time for another decision. Putting her in a nursing home where she would be safe, get constant care and not wander away. Was this the right decision I had to make?

In my mind the ancient saying kept repeating itself, I had to convince myself that it was for the best, so that the rest of the family could get on with their lives. I went to see a counselor and she advised me that she should be placed in a nursing home. The decision was the most heart wrenching one, but right or wrong I would have to live with it the rest of my life.

In December of the same year Jim was in Leffests General Hospital for eight days under the care of our family doctor. The doctor said that Jim lungs couldn't take much more of his constantly getting Pneumonia. He suggested that he should go on disability from his job. Jim worked nights at Continental Bakery in Queens, New York. It took another year and Jim went on disability in June of 1976

I Had a Dream About My Father 1975 September

I remember in September of 1975 I had a dream that made me wonder if I did the right thing by placing my mother in the nursing home.

In the dream my father was sitting in the first row of the funeral parlor and asked me to bring my mother to him before the Holidays, I said that I wasn't sure because I had too many things to do. I sort of brushed him off and told him I didn't have much time but I would see if I could.

That was when I woke up. Going to work the next day my co- worker and friend Josie knew that I was upset and I told her about the dream. She said it's only a dream. We continued to work that day and knowing that my mother was in the nursing home and in a safe place I put the dream in the back of my mind.

What happened next and still till today is mystery in my mind and can't be explained, only as a coincidence.

My Mother died on a Monday November 24 1975 just three days before Thanksgiving.

It so happened that the funeral parlor was located near my mother's house that my father had built for her when they were married. On the way there and before we went into the funeral parlor you could see the house which was in flames. When my father sold the house against her wishes she said she would burn it. Instead of going in the funeral parlor my sisters and brothers watched the flames of my parent's house and where we were born in, *burning.* How final when one generation finished, and we all became orphans. After the funeral we realized that Life has its mysterious ways of ending. Mom's wishes came true and Dad had Mom with him for the Holidays.

When I read or hear of a person that has a family member with Alzheimer's it brings back a flood of memories that I went through with Mom. I still think about the decision I made and if it was right. I'll never know but I hope it will never happen to my children, and for them to be burdened with making those decisions.

Sometimes we get to be happy about certain things. A new Grandson, James Joseph Maurin, born November 11, 1975 named after Jim. This made him happy that he had a namesake.

Jim Went Out on Disability 1976-1977

Following my Mom's passing I went to work for a little dress shop near my home. The shop was owned by an elderly couple and put me in charge of running the place. Her husband did the pressing of the garments and his wife only wanted to work on the sewing machine. I was accountable for opening and close the shop. I did the hiring and dismissing of operators, calling the manufacturer and establishing a price on a garment, also setting a shipping date. There were about twenty five operators in the shop and that sometimes caused a problem. One or two wanted to choose the section of the dress they wanted to work on for the day. There was one that was an experienced operator and in the morning I would give her an option between two sections. This

98

always worked, and I kept her busy all day. The job didn't last very long because the hours were getting longer, especially on shipping days I would get home later than usual. That was when I realized that maybe it was time after 24 years in the garment industry to change careers.

That year Jim was having trouble catching his breath, he couldn't walk more than a block and he would be out of breath. He was under the doctor's care and most of the time had to go for breathing treatments.

This went on for another year and the doctor said he should go on disability, which he did in 1976. Working nights in the winter for 26 years took its toll.

The most Joyful thing that happened, my daughter Nancy had a beautiful daughter Maria Elena Maurin on September 16, 1977. She was born three days before her mother's birthday. Now we had four grandchildren. Both my daughters have the perfect family, a boy and girl each.

**(From Left to Right: Thomas, Tina (top), James and
Maria Up front)**

Chapter Thirteen

A New Career

1978

After leaving the garment industry I decided that I would like to try a different career. At the time Mayor La Guardia of New York City opened up Puerto Rico and the garment industry went south. This was the demise of the garment industry and after 24 years in the industry I seen the writing on the wall.

Again I had to leave my job because I wanted to work half days to be with Jim. I applied for a job in food service in the Board of Education, and I would only work half days. I went to work at, *Franklin K Lane High School the school that I had to leave in 1939, to take care of my baby brother Frankie.*

This worked out well because Jim would be up all night and slept in the morning. He also went to the Veterans Hospital for his medication. He regained some of his strength and he didn't get out of breath as often.

Our routine was working out well and Jim started to do little things around the house and also loved to take pictures of the family.

Our First Trip to Italy 1979

One day Jim said that he wanted to take pictures of where his father was born in Sicily and maybe we should go to Italy. I must say that I was very happy and to tell the truth I really wanted to go. So in 1979 we booked a trip with Perrello Tours. It was a bit scary and I was apprehensive about how it would affect Jim's health. We didn't know if he could make the trip but the doctor said he could go.

On our first trip to Italy we knew that we were going to come back and really see all of Italy. I felt that a whole new world opened up for Jim and me. I remember that he was feeling better when he asked if there was a place where we could buy some Italian figs. In Rome we found a building that had little booths in it. On the Via Gracia, it is sort of a Walmart with all the different booths that sold: produce, cheese, meats, flowers and all things that are needed for the day.

In Italy the women plan their meals of the day because they prepare only fresh food every day. They only have small refrigerators and hardly any freezers.

This is one of the incidents, I will never forget, going to the booth that had fruits and vegetables and met the proprietor and asked him in Sicilian, that my husband wanted some fresh figs. The minute I spoke, he knew I was Sicilian and wanted to know what Providence I was from. I told him I was from America but learned to speak the language because my grandparents insisted when we were small that we learned the language. At that time I had not used it since I was sixteen but to my surprise he understood what I wanted. He took two fig leafs and put about a dozen figs in and gave them to me. I asked him in Sicilian *quantu da dari and he replied signora pi lei e' un regalo, quannu ritorna a Roma mi paga* and I said *Grazie.* (Translation)   *how much did I own him.* He answered, *for you it's a gift and when you come back to Rome you can pay me.*

One of the most memorable places of Jims' and mine was the Island of Capri. We had an afternoon on our own to explore the island. We came to this little town high up in the mountain with its small alleyways. Most were paved with ceramic tiles even the gates to their houses were tiled. Not plain tiles but designed in bright colorful flowers, all kinds of fish and intricate patterns. The roads are small for any cars to go into town only a small bus would take people outside of town. In the small Piazza there was a little Catholic Church and the only other building with the little booths where the natives sold food and ceramics. Jim went up to the Bell Tower high in the mountain and I went shopping for ceramics which *I still have and use.* When Jim got back to the Piazza we smelled food cooking and made us aware that it was time for lunch. In one of little booths, this woman was making one of the food that grandmother used to make. *Zucchini it's the recipe that is in the beginning of the book.* We bought two sandwiches and some peaches and a bottle of

Fresca bubbly wine and sat on the church steps and had our lunch in the most romantic island in the world.

(Picture of Capri)

That night we were to dinner with another couple, Audrey and Nelson who were on the same tour. They were from Manchester England. Audrey and I decided that we wanted to go swimming. So the next day we took the small bus to the Marina Piccolo *a small beach in the mountains.* It was sort of a private beach. The temperature of water was like a warm bath and you could see the pebbles on the bottom of the water. The most fascinating thing was swimming through the rock archers in the water.

We also had many more experiences with them.

Another night at two in the morning we came back to the hotel and we got stuck in one of the small elevator between floors. Audrey was claustrophobic and was getting panicky. We banged and shouted and someone came to get us out. They gave us a stool but Audrey couldn't climb up so Jim and Nelson had to lift her and she landed like a whale on the next floor. We laughed the whole night.

When we were in Venice with them we took a boat taxi to Maruno, famous in the world for glass blowing. They had a gift shop and Audrey bought a glass Dolphin. Well, they asked her if she wanted it shipped and she said no and carried it. On the way she dropped it and it broke into a million pieces. It was a good thing we were still on the premises. They were very gracious and told her that they would replace it and they would ship it to her home. This time she agreed. Sometimes I wonder if they ever remember the fun we had.

Our Second Trip to Italy 1982

We decided that we would go back to Italy again, this time we would take the southern route to Sicily, so we could find where our parents were from. Both our parents came from Sicily. In Rome we went to see our favorite person, the man who gave us the figs at the fruit booth at the Via Garcia. We had to go back and pay him for the figs. We didn't think he would remember us but when he saw us he said In Sicilian, *Senoia, it is almost four years since you were here.* I couldn't believe that he recognized us after so many years. He also said that he knew that we would be back to Rome for some figs. This time I told him that he had to take the money or otherwise we wouldn't take the figs.

Sometimes I wonder if I would go back to Rome if he would know me it's been a long time and I am older.

The thrill of my life was, when we went to the Vatican for Sunday Mass. The church was very crowded and everyone was standing *no seats in the church*. When we walked in we saw 22 bishops, on the marble floor with their arms stretched out to form a cross. The music was playing and all of a sudden a procession and Pope John Paul came in. I was standing first in the aisle and he smiled and his robe rubbed against my arm. I cannot express the feeling but when I think about it, how grateful and blessed I was to see him in person. The Mass was quite long but it was the best that I had ever seen in my life time.

He consecrated the future Cardinals and gave us a memory we never forgot.

In my life time, faith has given me all the dreams I had when I was young. They were only dreams which at that time were dreams that would never happen. While on this tour we visited many other places which filled one of my albums.

Back to Work and Offer I Couldn't Refuse 1982

When we got back to the states I found out our food service union District Council 37, made an offer I couldn't refuse. It was to go to college and get my Applied Science degree in Food Service by going to college. Our group consisted of personnel from other schools in the same class. We became a special group which grew into an extended family. We would get together and help each other with our class work. Most of us made the Dean's list and before we realized, it was Graduation day in June 1984.

In September of '84 after graduation, I was assigned to manage The Queens School for Career Development and only worked there about six month and served some handicap children for lunch. The only problem was that I had to travel longer to reach the school and would get home later and didn't have enough time with Jim. This is a letter that the Assistant Principal sent to me and my supervisor. I didn't realize that he really appreciated my work with the students.

NEW YORK CITY
BOARD OF EDUCATION

142-10 Linden Blvd.
Jamaica, N. Y. 11436

(718) 529-5400

Dennis J. Durkin
Principal

QUEENS SCHOOL FOR
CAREER DEVELOPMENT

September 26, 1984

Mrs. E. Zung
Newton High School
School Cafeteria
48-01 90th Street
Elmhurst, N.Y. 11373

Dear Mrs. Zung:

I am writing to you to thank you for assigning Tina Gulino to our school, even though it was only a brief assignment.

During her stay with us, Ms. Gulino proved to be of optium value to our school program. As you are probably aware, our school was just recently assigned to former JHS 142 building. The opening days of school were hectic, and students were unfamiliar with the new surroundings.

Ms. Gulino and the lunchroom staff performed heroically in the first days, insuring each child with breakfast and lunch. This was a major factor in setting the tone of the school. I wish Ms. Gulino the best of luck and hope that you appreciate her as much as we did.

Sincerely,

Allan Bauer
Allan Bauer
Assistant Principal
(Interim Acting)

Our Last Trip to Italy 1985

Jim wanted to go back to Europe to follow the route that the Army took during the war. TWA had a tour that went to most of the places that Jim was in during World War II. We didn't landed in Le Havre in France where Jim landed by ship in 1943, but we did landed in Amsterdam, Holland.

The trip took 21 days but Jim recalled some things that happened when he was there. We stayed in Holland for three days. We took the tour that would bring us nearer to the route that the army took. I remember in one of his letters telling me about the dikes and how they had to go through them and how wet they were, *there was no one to put their finger into the dike to stop the water.* They were on their way to meet with the rest of the First army. Jim was a messenger or scout who would reconnaissance the movements of the enemy territory before the troops were sent in. He was in the 413 division of the 104th Infantry. The Timber Wolf is the patch of a gray Timber Wolf signifying howling in the night at the moon. The Division was under Major Ger. Terry Allen and they fought the enemy at night, they were night fighters.

The trip took us down the Rhine into Cologne. When we arrived in Cologne there were many reminders of what the war did to the Cathedral of Cologne. There were gaping holes in the stones of the walls of the Cathedral. There were many towns that they went through but we didn't get to see them. The only one that made an impression was the little town called Merkin, where they fought on December 18-19 in 1944.

Nazis Hitting Hard—
Our GI Joe Backs Up

By GRAHAM MILLER
(Staff Correspondent of The News)

With U. S. 1st Army in Belgium, Dec. 17 (Delayed).—
The aim and scope of the German counteroffensive became
clearer tonight after a day of confused and fluid fighting
along a front of nearly 60 miles. This is big stuff.

The Germans are hitting us with several divisions, some
of them armored, and they are hitting us hard. Yesterday
they made jabs along the length of a line stretching from
Monschau, southeast of Aachen, east of Luxembourg. Today
they began to exploit their initial penetrations. German
armor and infantry with air support are now thrusting deep
into our front. We lost several villages in the course of today's fighting and so far have not succeeded in stopping or
containing the enemy.

(Official Signal Corps Radiophoto via Acme Telephoto)

In the Thick of It. When this picture was taken,
the 104th Division of Yank
1st Army was mopping up in Merken, Germany, after its capture.
Yesterday, because of a blackout in the news from this same front,
it was not known whether Merken has been retaken by Nazi
counteroffensive. Yanks lashed back in a great battle. —*Story on p. 2*

Dec 18+19

(Picture of where they fought.)

boys...
wash suits
1.98

Easy to launder, fine cot
fabrics! Smartly styled v
solid color shorts in bro
blue or tan with white shi
Suspender style. Sizes 3 t

Cordaroy
in Suits
2.98

Toddler
Cotton

skirt, Blue,
es 3 to 6X.

Pastel shor
shirt, Sizes

Belgians Flee Nazi Advanc

(Continued from page 8)

had been friendly with the Ame
cans and did not wish to suf
again at the hands of the Naz
These rear echelon units had
move back so rapidly that the
was no time to take personal b
longings, and Red Cross club
bile girls and Army nurses we
given orders to pack quickly, an
move further to the rear.

Harried to Pack.

I and other correspondents hu
ried to pack our belongings an
get our equipment in shape, re
luctantly leaving the billets whic
seemed almost like home.

Several Belgian friends came for
ward to bid me a sad farewell, and
several of them asked to be taken
along in our jeep, but we were fully
loaded and had to say no.

As I left, two women came for
ward to shake hands and wish us
"a bientoht," showing they knew
we would return.

But we can't deny that with our
having fallen back for the present
one segment of Belgium which the
1st Army liberated is once again
under Nazi control.

Sees Nazis Sealed Off.

Meanwhile, a lot of American
doughboys are slugging it out too
to toe with the best the Germans
can offer, and other doughboys are
moving into position to help them.

At least these American soldiers
said to me this afternoon "They'll
never believe this story back in th
states. It's a little hard for me to
believe it myself."

I can say with assurance that
the Germans won't get to Paris by
Christmas or even next Christmas
and though it may be several days
before the German thrust is sealed
off, Lieut. Gen. Hodges has the men
and equipment to do the job.

U.S. Infantrymen Rise Up From Cabbage Patch

By GRAHAM MILLER
(Staff Correspondent of The News)

With U. S. 1st Army Troops Before-Schophoven, Germany, Dec. 11.—We are dug in tonight outside Schophoven after being pinched out of Pier, which we reached yesterday. We had to get out of Pier because there were too many Germans with too many and too heavy guns for us to deal with at the moment.

Our infantry attacked Pier and took up positions in a factory on the outskirts, knocked loopholes in those walls still standing and organized bazooka teams and automatic fire to cover all approaches. But they didn't have any tank-destroyers with them and they didn't have much in the way of artillery support either, because the lay of the land was difficult.

Pretty soon German tanks rolled up and the bazookas opened fire. Some of our men who got back said those were the biggest tanks they had seen, the new Tiger Royals.

Bazooka Teams Leave.

The bazookas' shells bounced off their thick hides like dried peas, and the tanks, supported now by self-propelled guns, swung their turrets around in a casual sort of way and proceeded to demolish the factory. Our boys fought as long as they could, until they'd suffered evous casualties and the broken-arted bazooka teams had fired their last ineffectual rounds. Then they got out.

Today, from the top floor of a rickety shell-battered building in Inden which the 104th Division of Major Gen. Terry (Terrible Terry) Allen took after a brilliant attack a week ago, I watched the attack on Schophoven.

Ahead was open ground rising to a barely discernible ridge. There were cabbages all across this ground and beyond the ridge was Schophoven, apparently uninhabited and every detail crystal clear in the Marmtless noonday sun.

Markers for Airmen.

To the right was Pier, with smoke rising from it, and still farther to the right lay Merken. Our infantrymen, lying in foxholes scraped among the cabbages ahead, were waiting for the air corps to blast the town before they jumped off.

Lieut. Ben L. Nicoioni, a black-haired, good-looking young officer who used to spend a lot of time in New York and who spoke with nostalgia of happy times at the Club 18, was talking over a field telephone to batteries back of us. A few seconds later shells swished over our heads and vivid colored smoke began to drift over Schophoven. The shells were markers for the air corps.

We all looked at our watches and waited. But the smoke drifted away and the planes didn't show up. Then over another phone came information that the air corps

needed more time but would with us at such and such an ho and could they please have sme five minutes before that time.

It was as casual and informal receiving a telephone call in a ho lobby that someone you had ranged to dine with would be a f minutes late but would you ple order two dry Martinis.

So we waited and laid the sm and then the planes came. T were dive-bombers and they ph meted out of that blue sky at awful speed just as if they w eager to demonstrate that t were sorry to have kept us wait Our artillery opened up at same time.

Curtained by this fire and de struction, the infantrymen rose from the cabbage patches and be gan to move forward. But there were winking flashes through the smoke on the other side and enemy shells began to reach out for us.

Call for Medics.

The rickety old building we were in shook and trembled. From the street below our observation win dow, where a GI had been hit in the leg by a splinter, came a cry for the medics.

We clattered noisily down the crazy stairs and sat in the base ment.

"If anybody sheeted that top floor would fall off," said Lieut. Raymond C. Regan of 10 E. Raleigh Ave., West New Brighton, Staten Island. "There's nothing we can do up there for a little while, anyway, so we might as well be comfortable."

And we were, too.

Yardley Helps Canad

Later, we learned that Brig
wanted him in his undercover, ho
came the report from the unde
heard of it, recalled the Black C
thumbs down. Then up popped
aiding the Dominion's military in
Back came the story to the cap
been tipped off by Stimson that

So far as we've been able to l
Chamber, neither the Canadians
Yardley. Incidentally, after his
Washington conference, he had
Medal by the late Secretary of W
the citation, which diplomatically
on the Jap dispatches from Tokyo
ton.

So we set out on a search to
expert has been doing of late.

We discovered Major Yardle
the food division of OPA's We
spare time thinking of plots for
la the height of something or ot

25

Cologne Saints Gaze On Two Dead Yanks

By GRAHAM MILLER

(Staff Correspondent of The News)

Cologne, March 7.—They were bringing two dead GIs around the Cathedral in Cologne when I reached it this morning. They both lay face downward, covered by blankets, their feet sticking out beyond the litters over the front of the jeep.

One of them was wearing spurs fastened eternally onto his combat boots, and somehow the sight of these spurs seemed to make the spectacle of those two American soldiers—among the last to be killed on this side of the Rhine—all the more poignant.

You could almost see the sort of man the one with the spurs had been: A tall, laughing GI, maybe from Texas or Arizona, who had found these German spurs somewhere and had fastened them on his combat boots and laughed and joked with the rest of his platoon of Major Gen. Terry Allen's 104th (Timberwolf) Division as they fought their way farther towards the Rhine.

There's a smoking tank—not one of ours—a Tiger Royal standing almost in line with the western facade of the Cathedral. The entire hall is almost red hot and from the apertures and gun ports in its steel hide there are still a few flickering flames.

Every now and then machine-gun bullets explode inside it with a curious muffled report that gives the impression of small arms fire at a distance, but the memorable thing about that tank and the horrible thing about it is the curious smell of its smoke as it drifts across the open square.

It catches you at the back of the nostrils and suddenly you want to be sick, for the smell is the smell of roasting flesh.

Twenty yards away is another tank, one of ours, and standing around it are some Joes who have just found some wine.

The slim, delicately shaped bock bottles with their gaudy labels look strange when gripped by these battle-calloused hands. It's normally the sort of wine that's served under indirect lighting by obsequious waiters and which costs you $8 a crack.

It hasn't cost these Joes even so much as a by-your-leave, and one of them bawls out, "Come and have a drink, correspondent. We've just opened the bar."

Overshadowing everything is the Cathedral. It stands there pitted by bomb splinters, most of its roof tiles blown away, but otherwise unharmed. It's so big and its twin spires are so austere and so beautiful and so miraculously dominating all the ugliness that you almost find yourself talking loudly in self-defense, like a child at a party.

The saints look down undamaged from their niches, stony-eyed and beautifully carved by craftsmen dead these hundreds of years. In the Lady Chapel a GI has just risen from his knees. He wears the patch of the 104th Division and his eyes look startlingly blue against his grimy face and three-day growth of beard. He's maybe 22 and, with a shattering simplicity, he replies to your question of what do you think of the Cathedral:

"I was just thanking God for being alive."

Cologne's Fall Expected Soon, Miller Reports

By GRAHAM MILLER

(Staff Correspondent of The News)

With U. S. 1st Army Troops Before Cologne, March 4.—Cologne is tottering to its fall tonight and fighting within the city itself can be expected soon. After a day of unceasing rain, troops of Major Gen. Terry Allen's 104th (Timberwolf) Division are fighting in the little town of Frechen, within two miles of Cologne proper.

It's hard fighting, and the terrain is of advantage to the enemy.

Major Gen. Terry Allen.
Two miles from Cologne.

This is a squalid area of slag heaps and coal mines. The doughboys have to move along the causeways between the slag heaps which the enemy has had time to cover with artillery and mortars.

Frechen was attacked from three directions—north, south and west—and tanks of Major Gen. Maurice Rose's 3d Armored Division, which has been spearheading our infantry all through this offensive, exchanged shot for shot with German artillery during this entire gloomy day.

This morning the northern end of the town was cleared as far as the main Cologne-Duren road which cuts Frechen in half. In the southern half the fighting is still going on, with the Germans hanging on bitterly to smashed houses and street intersections, even with tank destroyers smashing shell after shell into the buildings above them.

The only people who are surrendering are Hitler's eager Volkstormers who, when given half a chance, throw away their arms, tear off their brassards and pile into trucks which take them back to our cages.

From the point before Cologne, Al Newman, Newsweek war correspondent, sends this story of a foxhole division and a fight by night.

Maj. Gen. Terry de la Mesa Allen, once the famous commander of the First Division of North African fame, recently popped up in the thickest of the fighting on the western front with his new division—the 104th, which wears a shoulder patch depicting a gray timber wolf howling at a nonexistent moon in a green sky. They were in fast company, for to their south at some of the greatest divisions of the United States Army—the First, Third Armored, Ninth, and Fourth.

Until they saw action in October with the Canadians north of Antwerp, the 104th had never even undergone an air raid. The first division to land directly at Cherbourg, they missed Britain completely.

But by this third week of the big push, it became apparent that Terry Allen had trained a very good division indeed. Jumping off on Nov. 16 into the long-disputed town of Stolberg, they had fought their way to the bloody yard over the ridge into Eschweiler, turned east to Weisweiler, then southeast to Inden.

Nightmares at Arms: Allen fought his timber wolves some new tricks along with the old, for as German on their sector have discovered, the 104th is a body of night-fighting specialists. Strangely enough, this is a little-developed technique in modern warfare, for most commanders fear mixups which result in ...

U.S. Infantrymen Rise Up From Cabbage Patch

By GRAHAM MILLER
(Staff Correspondent of The News)

With U. S. 1st Army Troops Before Schophoven, Germany, Dec. 11.—We are dug in tonight outside Schophoven after being pinched out of Pier, which we reached yesterday. We had to get out of Pier because there were too many Germans with too many and too heavy guns for us to deal with at the moment.

Our infantry attacked Pier and took up positions in a factory on the outskirts, knocked loopholes in those walls still standing and organized bazooka teams and automatic fire to cover all approaches. But they didn't have any tank-destroyers with them, and they didn't have much in the way of artillery support either, because the lay of the land was difficult.

Pretty soon German tanks rolled up and the bazookas opened fire. Some of our men who got back said those were the biggest tanks they had seen, the new Tiger Royals.

Bazooka Teams Leave.

The bazookas' shells bounced off their thick hides like dried peas, and the tanks, supported now by self-propelled guns, swung their turrets around in a casual sort of way and proceeded to demolish the factory. Our boys fought as long as they could, until they'd suffered grievous casualties and the broken-hearted bazooka teams had fired their last ineffectual rounds. Then they got out.

Today, from the top floor of a rickety shell-battered building in Inden which the 104th Division of Major Gen. Terry (Terrible Terry) Allen took after a brilliant attack a week ago, I watched the attack on Schophoven.

Ahead was open ground rising to a barely discernible ridge. There were cabbages all across this ground and beyond the ridge was Schophoven, apparently uninhabited and every detail crystal clear in the warmthless noonday sun.

Markers for Airmen.

To the right was Pier, with smoke rising from it, and still farther to the right lay Merken. Our infantrymen, lying in foxholes scraped among the cabbages ahead, were waiting for the air corps to blast the town before they jumped off.

Lieut. Ben L. Nicolosi, a black-haired, good-looking young officer who used to spend a lot of time in New York and who spoke with nostalgia of happy times at the Club 18, was talking over a field telephone to batteries back of us. A few seconds later shells swished over our heads and vivid colored smoke began to drift over Schophoven. The shells were markers for the air corps.

We all looked at our watches and waited. But the smoke drifted away and the planes didn't show up. Then over another phone came information that the air corps

needed more time but would be with us at such and such an hour and could they please have smoke five minutes before that time.

It was as casual and informal as receiving a telephone call in a hotel lobby that someone you had arranged to dine with would be a few minutes late but would you please order two dry Martinis.

So we waited and laid the smoke and then the planes came. They were dive-bombers and they plummeted out of that blue sky at an awful speed just as if they were eager to demonstrate that they were sorry to have kept us waiting.

Our artillery opened up at the same time.

Curtained by this fire and destruction, the infantrymen rose from the cabbage patches and began to move forward. But there were winking flashes through the smoke on the other side and enemy shells began to reach out for us.

Call for Medics.

The rickety old building we were in shook and trembled. From the street below our observation window, where a GI had been hit in the leg by a splinter, came a cry for the medics.

We clattered noisily down the crazy stairs and sat in the basement.

"If anybody sneezed that top floor would fall off," said Lieut. Raymond C. Regan of 10 E. Raleigh Ave., West New Brighton, Staten Island. "There's nothing we can do up there for a little while, anyway, so we might as well be comfortable."

And we were, too.

Belgians Flee Nazi Advance

(Continued from page 2)

had been friendly with the Americans and did not wish to suffer again at the hands of the Nazis.

These rear echelon units had to move back so rapidly that there was no time to take personal belongings, and Red Cross clubmobile girls and Army nurses were given orders to pack quickly and move farther to the rear.

Hurried to Pack.

I and other correspondents hurried to pack our belongings and get our equipment in shape, reluctantly leaving the billets which seemed almost like home.

Several Belgian friends came forward to bid me a sad farewell, and several of them asked to be taken along in our jeep, but we were fully loaded and had to say no.

As I left, two women came forward to shake hands and wish us "a bientoto," showing they knew we would return.

But we can't deny that with our having fallen back for the present one segment of Belgium which the 1st Army liberated is once again under Nazi control.

Sees Nazis Sealed Off.

Meanwhile, a lot of American doughboys are slugging it out toe to toe with the best the Germans can offer, and other doughboys are moving into position to help them.

At least three American soldiers said to me this afternoon "they'll never believe this story back in the states. It's a little hard for me to believe it myself."

I can say with assurance that the Germans won't get to Paris this Christmas or even next Christmas, and though it may be several days before the German thrust is sealed off, Lieut. Gen. Hodges has the men and equipment to do the job.

We continued our trip and went down the Rhine to Heidelberg and to Switzerland for three days. We stood at the Grand Hotel Europe on the fourth floor. The next morning when we opened our balcony door we viewed the most spectacular site The Alps the Mountains of Switzerland.

Then through Rome and then into southern France and up to northern Calais and took the *hydrofoil, a boat that runs* on *top of water)* to England and it landed on the shore of the White Cliff of Dover. We went on to London where Jim was sent to a hospital when he had developed Pneumonia during the war. That was our last trip out of the country.

Chapter Fourteen

An Interview for a New Job

1986

After coming home from our long trip and seeing so many countries we were glad to be home with our family.

While talking with my sister Ann whom was a bookkeeper at Richmond Hill High School, she mentioned there was an opening for a Para Professional Teacher, I called and received a date for my interview.

March 1986

Here, I was a woman who had two careers, who went to college when most people my age were getting ready for retirement. I was a loving wife, mother and grandmother, who would always be needed by my family and friends. I needed more! I wasn't ready for retirement, what was I getting into. Questions, oh so many, I asked myself let the questions wait, here I was and there was no turning back. Anyway, I may not even get the job!

I walked into the principal office, a beautiful room with soft walnut paneled walls, comfortable chairs, and a table that was at least ten feet long and intimidating.

After our introductions we all sat at one end of the table, the principal, assistant principal and a student counselor. My adrenaline started to work overtime. The same question flashed in my mind only this time they were interrupted by someone else, with a new set of questions. Why did I want this job? It offered oh, so many problems with special teenagers. Next question, how would I handle these complex problems?

(Ed) Emotionally Disabled, (ADHD) Attention Deficit Hyperactive Disorder, (EMR) Educable Mentally Retarded, (L D) Learning Disabled. I would learn so more about their titles. I answered the questions with all the emotions I felt about my own children. My own first granddaughter, Tina, with a handicap, Dyslexia, remembering what my daughter Angela and granddaughter had to go through to overcome this handicap. She was a little girl, bright and normal in every way, but had a problem with her writing. When tested, what her eyes saw her hand reversed. This one learning disability was with her eye and hand coordination. How many hours they worked together to correct this condition. *She is now a Doctor of Chiropractic, with her professional* life *intact.* As you can imagine, I did get the job.

Special Education Beginning of 1986

Richmond Hill H.S. had its own Special Education department and was independent of the mainstream classes. They had a teacher for each subject; this gave the students individual attention in the major subjects. The principle allowed us to teach the students different subjects that would give them extra credits, subjects that for some students it would mean the difference between graduation or not.

I was asked if I would implement a Food Service Program for the students since I had a background of working in food service for Broad of Education and an Associate Degree in Food Service Management. I informed the students that they would work in the cafeteria for extra credit. This would also give them an idea of how the cafeteria worked; the preparation of food, how to serve, clean up, etc.

This school had three lunch periods. I recruited six students for each period, made a schedule of what period everyone would work and supervised the entire operation. At the end of the week, I would have a class where we reviewed what they had accomplished. They received a grade for the quality of their work. Every other week, a test was given on what they had learned about sanitation, nutrition and the handling of food. At end of the term their assignment was to write a small paper on what they learned and how they felt about the program. These students also acquired interpersonal relationship skills with cafeteria staff and the faculty.

Most said, they didn't realize how much work went into preparing lunch for the students, others said, they would like to get a job in food service. There was a senior whose family was receiving public assistance; and after his experience in the program, he decided that he was interested in getting a job upon graduation in a School Food Service department. He was an excellent student and a conscientious worker. The school happened to have a position available and with a little help from me and the food service manager, he was hired.

As of this writing, Fernando B. is married and has been employed in the School Food Service. He is not receiving Public assistance any longer and is earning a substantial salary.

Another class that I loved was being an assistant to Mr. David Chin in the wood working shop. His class was one of the most productive of all the classes. He would teach the students and I the rules of safety and how to use all the power tools. I had worked with my husband when we built our house, but this was different. These were commercial tools. I took to it like a duck takes to water. The students enjoyed working with me and I with them.

We created things that we could use-wooden trays, bread boxes, shelves, cutting boards and clocks. I had free rein in the shop. Most of the time the periods were never long enough for the students and me.

I never had any problems with the students, everyone did their work and we all were challenged to do something else. David was to me a Mentor, the students loved him and so did I.

David and his family have kept in touch at Christmas time for the past 25 years.

Much to my regret I had to leave this job, because Jim wanted to move to our house in Palenville, New York. Jim still would get days when he couldn't breathe too well and couldn't do anything; maybe the fresh air would be better for his condition, he had a very bad case of Asthma. It was a sacrifice on my part because I was about to join the United Teachers Association. *Sometimes in Life you have to do whatever is right for the person you love.* Things change and most of the time for the best. What happened next was we sold the house in Woodhaven after living in it for 31 years. Our daughters were married from the house. Oh, so many memories.

To whom it may concern;

I have been a high school industrial arts/technology teacher working with the special ed. population for over 18 years at Richmond Hill. I have had several paraprofessionals assisting my classes and me over the years. However, no one has come close to the ability and quality of the job performed by Tina Gulino.

Tina performed admirably in what has been typified as a " man's world ". She took an active part in the day to day operation of the woodworking classes. She was eager and quick to learn the operation of all the tools and equipment in the shop. She was just as eager to aid the students in their work once she became familiar with the tools. The students looked upon her with awe and amazement. Her involvement in all facets of the shop served as an inspiration to the students. Her active presence in the shop help to break down many gender and age stereotypes perceived by the students and even myself.

Her influence on the students went beyond the mechanical skills that she shared with the students. Tina was and still is a very caring and nurturing person. She helped to calm and reassure many a troubled special ed. student as only a caring and experienced professional could. In return, the students treated her with respect and trust, which are qualities not easily earned by educators today.

Even though Tina left Richmond Hill H.S. about 8 years ago, she is still remembered fondly to this day. In the years preceding her arrival and in the years since her departure, I have not had a paraprofessional who has come close to Tina's abilities and devotion. She is the standard by which I measure all other paraprofessionals and educators. I know that no matter what professional road that Tina takes, she will do her best in all endeavors.

Sincerely,

David Chin

Another Change 1987

Jim's older brother Vinny was in the city in a nursing home and had no one to take care of him. We felt that we should take him to one of the nursing homes upstate so we could visit him. He was so happy that we were going to live upstate and he was included in our plans.

119

Everything was going fine except that I couldn't adjust to being retired. Who am I? I sit here, looking at the soaps wondering why I am doing this. A year ago we moved to our house in Palenville and it was a long winter. Well the winter has passed and again I wasn't ready for retirement. Being home for almost a year and missed my friends at Richmond Hill High School. I wrote to one of my closest friends, Sandy.

Dear Sandy,

It's time to write you a letter, but we have been busy with the house. It seems longer, yet there are days when I feel so desperate for all of you. I made new friends and everyday a few more. I need to get involved in something. I took a writing course at Columbia Greene Community College that summer, which was great. It helped me it made me loosen up a bit and put my thought on paper. I am determined to go back to work. It's funny how things happen in life. Our house needed the wood trim to be painted and one of my friends up here told me about this teacher who did painting in the summer when school was closed His name was Mr. Churchhill and he was the music teacher in Catskill High School. While he was painting the house he told me that they needed Subs at the school and would I like a job. It took quite a bit of talking to convince Jim that I would only work two or three days a week. I will keep you Posted.

Fondly Tina

A New Challenge – Para Professional Substitute Teacher 1988

Well, the winter had passed and Jim said yes I could take the job as a substitute teacher. I started working in the Catskill Central School District on March 22, 1988 and felt that I had a new lease on life. I recall my father had worked as a maintenance man in the school after he retired from the Post Office and there some people that knew me at the school plus I knew Mr. Churchhill. When we came up to live permanently in our home my two daughters were already living there. Since I had started to work at the school my three grandchildren, Thomas, James and Maria were in the Catskill School System and Tina was graduating from St. Pats High School. They were taking the bus to school, but grandma was driving to school. You can guess what took place, grandma became the school bus. There was only one thing wrong, the boys wanted to sit up front with me. Tom who was the oldest always pulled rank and got his way but Jim didn't like to argue so most of the time Tom sat up front.

Tom was the adventurous type and loved to climb mountains, go caving and belonged to the Civil Air Patrol. Tom is now a Park Police Officer in New York State and in the Air Force Reserve. He always knew what he wanted to do. Jim was the academic student, the only sport he loved was running, he was on the Track Team. He received a Regents Diploma in Spanish. He is in college studying Computer Engineering. Maria was interested in the school plays and had good grades.

She still loves her acting Hobby but became a License Massage Therapist.

Chapter Fifteen

Jim's New Project

1988

Jim had a new project that he wanted to do. He was going to build a deck off the kitchen. What a great idea, it would keep him busy and I was happy, doing what I loved to do, being with the students.

Jim felt a little better and found something he wanted to do but he had a challenge on his hands

It was spring and when a young man's fancy turns to love, he's not the only one. *It seems that every living creator in the world gets the love bug at this time of the year.* Jim had constructed the deck with four-by-four posts so that he could put a roof over part of the deck. This was putting a "For Rent" sign on all the post for all species of birds to inhabit.

Jim had hardly finished the deck when we had birds moving in on every post. He didn't mind them building their nests, but we had so many trees on the property, Oak, Hickory, Maple, Pine and others trees which could be used to make their nests in. Maybe they liked to be close to home where the other species were, like the Blue Jays who are scavengers and they would steal their eggs. They were safe on the deck.

Desperate for a solution to cover the post that was near the picnic table, Jim tied a red brick on the post. Not high enough the birds still built their nest. We wonder who was going to win, the birds or us. The birds kept Jim busy until he had another idea; he devised a screen to put around the post so that we could at least enjoy part of the deck. "Wrong again." It seemed that other birds had carte blanche to the other post. Every time we gathered at one section of the deck we had birds flying in our face. They would fly to the tree branch close to the deck, and angrily chirping as if to tell us to leave, for they had to sit on the nest to feed their young. Jim eventually put screens on all the posts, but I must admit that I missed some of the birds.

A New Wing on the House 1989

When we moved from Woodhaven we took with us an accumulation of what we had collected in the thirty years. Some things were collectable others were a combination of cutter that only had some emotional value. We had to make a decision of what to get rid of and what to keep. Jim said we need to extend the old garage if we were to keep what we loved. There was no doubt we needed more space. He also said it would add value to the house.

In this space of time I had seen a picture of in a magazine for an extension in the shape of a Gazebo to add to the house. This addition to the house also gave us a view of the mountains from the room.

We had put money away to go to Japan but Jim didn't feel well enough to travel anymore, so we used the money to build the garage and the Gazebo. I agreed with him and I didn't want to go also because I loved my job at school and things were going better with Jim's health.

In 1990 it seemed that I spoke to soon. In the beginning of the year Jim became ill with Bronchial Asthma. We went to the Veterans Hospital in Albany; they kept him in for three days, from January 25-27 and gave him medication and then he came home. It was a bad time of the year and he didn't recuperate as fast as possible. The garage and the Gazebo were finished and Jim could relax and take it easy. But... that didn't happen, in February on Valentine's Day we had to go to Columbia Greene Memorial Hospital; the medication that he received at the Veterans hospital disagreed with him. He was in the hospital for eight days. Our doctor changed his medication and he began feeling better.

It was now the end of the term and summer was upon us. Jim was glad to have me home all day. We would go shopping and go to Sears where Jim would always find another tool to buy for his work shop or for the garden, he loved his vegetable garden. One year he planted pumpkin seeds and it took over the entire garden; our grandchildren were happy about that. I, of course would see something for my kitchen, a new gadget to make cookies or a garlic press. Every day we would take a ride to a Mall or to Jim's favorite store, Sears.

We had another wonderful celebration that year. My daughter Angela and my granddaughter Tina graduated Columbia Greene Community College on the same day in June. Angela, my daughter became a registered nurse at age forty three. My granddaughter Tina graduated in Independent Studies. *She went on to graduated from Life College of Chiropractic with her Doctorate in Chiropractic.*

My Brother Joe Passed Away 1990

It was July of that year, when I called my brother Joe to hear how he was feeling. He was a diabetic and was having trouble with his eyes he was also on dialysis 3x a week now and he was depressed for quite a while. He told me that he had a pain in his back but otherwise he was OK. In the morning I got a call that he died the next morning. This was a shock because he had accepted his illness and his wife Marion took good care of him. He was only fifty seven years old. This brought back memories of when we were young and how close we were, and the time when my brothers helped my father build the house upstate. I grew up loving my brothers and their families; he died on July 1 1990.

Jim didn't come to the funeral because he wasn't feeling well and he had an attack of Asthma and couldn't catch his breath very well.

Some New Neighbors Down the Hill 1990

Down the hill from our house, we noticed that there were some people working on clearing the land. They were up from the city on weekends and holidays; this reminded Jim and I about the times when we would do the same. We watched from our house the progress that they were making. Soon there was three modular's standing.

I don't remember exactly how we met them. However, they became our extended Sicilian family. When we met I had tried to speak to them, but I could only remember bits and pieces. So many years had passed since I had used the Sicilian language.

Jim had never learned how to speak Sicilian, but he understood the language. His father had always spoken to his children in his native tongue. Now, to get back to the Sicilian family, we soon discovered that they were all related to each other. There was Aunt Rosa and her husband John, John's nephew Benny and his wife Maria, and Josephine, John's niece nicknamed (Pina) and her husband Joe. They were summer people, people who only came to Upstate NY during the summer usually. They all lived in the City near each other. All winter they would call and ask how the weather was. Sometimes they would come up in the winter, but most of the time it was their grown children that would come up to go skiing. When I wanted to know things about Sicily, I would call Pina, and she would tell me about the culture and the food. Most of all she would tell me about the ancient customs that she grew up with. Pina is like another daughter; she is educated in America and is very modern but still keeps her Sicilian customs. *While I was writing this book, she was the one that I would call to get the correct Sicilian words that I needed.* I thought I knew everything about my Sicilian customs, but I was surprised to find out about some things that are different. The way they cook certain foods, the way they shop for fresh food every day. Different customs were lost when our grandparents came to America. Till today, when they come up, it is a known fact that I have to go down the hill and eat their Sicilian food. I could never say that I couldn't go down and I never did say no... I always felt that I was back in Sicily enjoying the authentic foods.

Chapter Sixteen

This Was My Calling

1991

The year started out being very busy, I was working more than two or three days in a week and most of the teacher's requested me to take their classes when they were out. I recall one person, Ms. Janet Headley the Home Economics teacher. Anytime she was out, she made sure that I was available to take her classes. When she retired she made me a quilt with the names of my daughters and my grandchildren. I keep it on the wall in my sewing room. Her classes were up my alley, and many times her lesson plans included cooking or sewing with the students.

HCR 2 Box 468M
Cairo N. Y. 12413
March 1996

To Whom It May Concern:

It has been my privilege and pleasure to work closely with Tina Gulino for the past 8 years. Gulino has been a substitute in the Catskill Central High School for that amount of time. During her tenure here I have watched her handle difficult situations and difficult students with the expertise of a trained master teacher.

Gulino has taken over classes on long term assignments for teachers who were critically ill and dying. In these instances she has handled the students feelings and their work with sensitivity. She has developed lessons, when needed, staying within the curriculum of that course as if she were trained in that particular area.

Gulino has taken over classes on short term assignments for teachers who were ill or in crisis with the same sensitivity and expertise as she has in long term assignments with or without prepared lessons.

When she has been in for me she has been careful to learn how my classes are run and provided the consistency students need in order to learn effectively. Gulino has the ability to sense what students need and she is able to structure lessons to the mood of the class and the day so that time is not lost because of my absence. As my substitute she is invaluable to me because I know that when she is in for me she will treat my students with the respect they deserve and she will see to it that my classroom rules are followed. I am always sure that she will meet or exceed my expectations and that the students will have had valuable learning experiences when I am able to return to my duties. She has even provided grading for me during extended periods of my absence. In each case her grades have been accurate and sensitive to the student doing the work in subjective situations. Further Gulino has furnished feedback to me and to my students so that we all understand how she has made the necessary judgements.

In my opinion Gulino is already a teacher and should be recognized with the appropriate certification based on her on the job experiences and her living skills as a teacher and a nurturing person.

Sincerely,

Janice M. Headley
Home Economist
Catskill Senior High School

130

Jim didn't mind my subbing anymore because he would sleep late in the morning and I would be home by two thirty from school. I also was only ten minutes away from home if he needed me. He knew how much I loved being at school with the students and working one on one with some of them.

In May of that year I took over Mrs. "N's" French class. She went for an operation and asked me to take her classes. I had taken them every time she was absent and she always gave terrific lesson plans. This time it was quite different, I would have the class every day for a month or more. I knew all the students and they were great and made me feel I could do it. I was grateful that Jim and I had traveled to France and knew about the people and places. I had caught on to the language somewhat because I spoke Italian.

Every day after they finished their worksheets I would tell them a story about France and our experiences, in the little towns and the people, and food we encountered on our trip. One time our tour took us to a French restaurant and most of the people on the tour were looking forward to trying the Escargot. Jim and I in our lifetime had eaten escargot (snails). It was a Sicilian delicacy. When they served the escargot most of the people took one look and refused to eat them. Jim and I were sitting at the end of the table and some asked if anyone wanted them. We accepted them and enjoyed with garlic butter and French bread.

When Mrs. "N." came home from the hospital I would go over to her house after school and brought the work done from the day. She in turn would give me the new assignment; this went on for about two months.

131

There were times when the students would ask me to say something in Italian and then we would look up words in the French dictionary. The vowels in French are different but most of the time I would understand them.

What the students did or didn't realize was that I was getting a lesson in French. It was great to have the same students every day. Some students of this class were taking regents and this concerned me. Their Regents exams were going to take place when Mrs. "N" came back in a few weeks. Much to my surprise at the end of the term most all the students did very well on the regents.

CATSKILL HIGH SCHOOL

Office of the Guidance Department
CATSKILL SENIOR HIGH SCHOOL

343 West Main Street
CATSKILL, NEW YORK 12414
(518) 943-2345

March 6, 1996

To Whom it May Concern,

I have been acquainted with Tina Gulino for several years while she has been a substitute teacher at Catskill high School. She has taught for me on several occasions including approximately 2 months in 1991 while I was out due to back surgery.

Tina is always a dependable substitute. I know that my lesson plans will be carried out properly, that my classes will be well-controlled and that my students will be treated with respect. Furthermore, she is flexible and well-liked by students and teachers alike.

During the time that she was my long-term substitute, she went above and beyond her normal duties. She either came out to my house or called me everyday. She took a difficult situation for me and made it much easier.

Over the years, Tina has become considered as a regular member of the staff of our school and as one of our most preferred substitutes.

Sincerely,

Joyce Notarnicola
Joyce Notarnicola

Mrs. Pat Lewis and Karin Schmidt

In the fall of 1991 the Compensatory Reading teacher Mrs. Pat Lewis became ill and I was asked to take her classes. I had always taken her classes when she was absent and I enjoyed working with these special students. Mrs. Lewis was one of the best teachers in the school and I was happy to help her out. It turned out that I would have her classes from October 1991 until February of 1992. I'll never forget what happened that year. Mrs. Lewis was to return to work on a Monday and I had the students make a banner and cards to welcome her back but she passed away that weekend. That left me to explain to the class what happened. It was a bad time for all of us.

(Me and Karin)

Mr. Stickles, the principal asked me to stay on until they would get another reading teacher. He would send some new teachers to the class and then asked me what I thought of them. There was only one person that I thought would fit the position. When she came into the room she didn't talk to me.

She introduced herself to the students and talked to them. When she left Mr. Stickles asked me what I thought and I said she was the one. I soon found out that she was she was going to be the new reading teacher. The next time she came in we worked together until she took over the class. We became best friends and I felt that she was like one of my daughters. Karin taught me how the system worked and what had to be done at the end of a term and how to evaluate a student's work. In fact I always went to her when I had a problem at school. I adopted her as my other daughter.

She is still my daughter and she always calls from Florida. We still keep in touch and she calls me Mom.

Chapter Seventeen

Jim's Condition Never Resolved

1993

I went back to subbing for the rest of the year for another teacher, Jim was happy that I wasn't working every day. His condition was getting worse and he would be up all night. He kept getting medication from the V. A. Hospital in Albany but it didn't help much, it affected his blood pressure and enlarged his liver.

This year started out as bad as last year. To keep my sanity I started again to write in my journal. It's been awhile since I had time to write, so many things happened and so many problems.

Jim's disability started in 1946 when he was under our primary doctor Dr. E Irioro and every time he had an attack he would give him a shot of adrenaline.

When we lived in the city he started to go to the Veterans Hospital in New York City, but there were times when he needed help right away and we would go to the doctor or the nearest hospital. Jim was told by someone at the V A, that he should go and ask for D.I.C (Death Indemnity Compensation) we filled all the paper work and after they denied his request, we went back with more information and waited for another letter. This went on till the end of the year.

Entry in Journal February 9 1993

     I really have a lot on my mind today. Took Jim to the doctor yesterday and it doesn't look good. His pressure is 200/100 and he is full of water. This is because his liver is not functioning. The doctor said he should be in the hospital, but Jim refused. I can't blame him, he doesn't want to have any more tests done like the last time. The next ten days will tell the story. He has to take a high blood pressure pill and a diuretic pill. Maybe by some miracle his fluid will go down. I really feel it may go down. It's not going to be easy, he has to be on a strict diet, no salt or fats and low protein. I know it won't be easy but I am sure I can do it.*

     The diet didn't help much and his fluid still was high. On 2/24/93 Jim had a terrible night, in the morning I made him tea and toast and he took his pill. Last night he didn't eat very much I made him plain soup and pastine but he only ate a little of it. I really don't know what to do; he has a hard time breathing. I know he doesn't want to go to the hospital but he really needs help. *We are in charge of our bodies and sometimes we don't know when we need help. I could not make this decision.* I didn't have to make one anyway because I had to take him to the Kingston Hospital when he had a fever and it was serious. On that day the V. A. denied this claim again. We didn't have time to pay attention to putting in another claim. Jim's condition was getting critical and was in the Kingston Hospital. Our doctor Dr. Biddy as we called him (Dr. Bhitiyakul) said, that Jim was critical and didn't expect him to live. In the hospital he went through a tracheotomy. He was on a respirator in the I.C.U. and I was there every day at 8:30 AM until 5:30PM and sometimes even later. I spent most of my time watching as he labored to breathe. The nurses were there and gave him the care I couldn't at home. Every day there was a plus or minus on his condition. This stay was one of the longest that he had ever been in any hospital. He was there from 2/25/1993 to 3/25/1993. It was kind of a miracle that he survived what he went through. He even surprised the nurses and our doctor.

March 19 1993

Jim was still in the hospital and I had spent most of my time there and had to make some life threatening decisions. It was the day before my birthday and it was also a month that Jim was in the hospital and I had another decision to make. I was tired and worried of what the future held for us. Well, that night my two beautiful daughters were with me when I broke down, that was the first time that happened, but I guess they knew how much stress I was under.

The next day when I came home from the hospital I was asked to go to dinner at my daughter's house. My older daughter told me she had to pick up my granddaughter at the restaurant where she worked.

It was my surprise birthday dinner and all my children and grandchildren were there. I always knew that having two loving daughters and my adopted daughter Karin would pay off someday, when I needed some T.L.C. "Tender Loving Care." I'll never forget that birthday.

Jim Was Still Fighting His Condition

April 1993

Jim was happy to be home, but his health was still a problem. His lungs were clear and he could breathe a little better. The problem was his liver, it wasn't functioning properly and he would fill up with fluid. His stomach and feet were swollen and the doctor said it would affect his heart.

My husband came home and feeling a bit better, wants to do so many things around the house. After being home, he wanted to go shopping and wanted to get some patio blocks for the vegetable garden. He really wanted to do everything but he didn't have the strength to do heavy work. We didn't buy the blocks, I talked him out of it, saying, next month when he was feeling much better we would get them.

Entry in Journal April 23 1993

That night I wrote, I wonder what is going to happen and how he going to feel if the doctor tells him how sick he is. I don't even want to know, but maybe I should know in order so I can get my life in order. I have the feeling that the worst time is yet to come. I really thought it wouldn't end like this and I don't like it. I hope and pray that God or Saint Joseph can help him get better. *Just another miracle!* I guess if the weather gets better, so will he.

Entry in Journal May 11 1993

We went to the doctor yesterday. Jim only lost 1 lb of water weight. The doctor discussed his condition, and Jim decided that he didn't want the shunt, because he would have to stay 4-5 days in the hospital to be monitored and he didn't want that. The doctor gave him another pill to take to get rid of more water. Jim was a little depressed because he wants to get better faster and this problem will take longer. I sort of felt better after talking to the doctor. He thinks in time and with no other complications, he will get better. I hope he is right. I don't think Jim has the patience though. The only thing we have to worry about is if the water gets to his lungs.

Entry in Journal June 11 1993

Here we go again, Jim was up all night, he was sick to his stomach. He threw up this morning maybe the pills were making him sick. I called Angela, my daughter the nurse. She came over and took his temperature and it was normal. She listened to his chest and she said it wasn't too bad.

I really was thinking of staying home, but he said he would be OK, he felt better. I will go home at lunch time to check on him and make him some soup with baby pasta. He worked in the garden yesterday and he did too much. His mind wants to do too much but his body is too weak.

Entry in Journal June 14 1993

I guess I am feeling sorry for myself today. The thought of being home all summer and worrying about Jim and making sure he doesn't do too much is going to be a job. Anyway, this weekend Jim was feeling a little better and I am trying to take one day at a time. Some days I feel like running away from it all. I would like to go away by myself and not deal with what is coming. I never knew about how I would cope with this situation, Not

Good! I feel that all Jim and I have done... is it really worth it? Maybe I should have been different when I was young. I should have done things different and not worry about what I had to do for everybody. I don't know what I am writing about, but like everything that has happened I probably would do the same thing over again. Whatever Life has in store for me I will COPE!

September, 1993

The summer went by and Jim was feeling better but still had a problem with his liver and the fluid in his body. I decided that I would go back to work. On the fourth day of school I received a call, and was asked if I could come in for the afternoon for Mr. Churchill's music class. This was one of my favorite classes and the class would always sing for me. It so happened that the Music Class was going to put on a play in April of 1994, it was going to be "My Fair Lady". Mrs. Churchill whom is the Gym teacher in the middle school and who is in charge of the props for the play asked me if I would help make the hats for the play. This was right up my alley! For most of my life I made most of my hats. I had to make about twenty one hats and this was a challenge, which I enjoyed doing. The play was one of the best that the school had ever put on. *I really feel that it isn't easy for the students with their curriculum and activities that they make time to put on a play.*

The Beginning of School Year September 1993

Jim wasn't happy about me going back to subbing, but I was! Our routine when I was home was that Jim would sleep until eleven or twelve and I couldn't make any noise. I convinced him that I wouldn't work every day and I would be home by 2:30. The students were glad to see me and so was I to see them. I also felt at home with the students and teachers. There were two teachers that made me feel at ease when I first started to sub; Annie Mac, the Librarian and Lorraine F. a great English teacher. As time went on I got to know and grew fond of most all of them. I could always count on Annie Mac for information on Jim's condition. I remember one time in particular when Jim was searching for more information on Chronic Liver Disease. She looked it up on the computer in school and made copies for Jim. I took them home to read with Jim. They were very informative and I highlighted the important parts. We also took copies to show his doctor and thought maybe he could do something to bring down stomach. It didn't work.

I needed to express my feelings so I started to write in my journal again about his bad days. Jim started to talk about what happened during the war and so I also put in another claim for all his VA files when he was in the war.

At the same time Jim's, brother Vinny whom was in the Nursing Home in Catskill since 1987, was sent to the hospital for a Hernia operation. That was another problem that Jim couldn't handle. Most of the time, if Vinny had a problem at the nursing home, they would call me and they knew that Jim was ill; Vinny came through the operation fine, he missed his brother not coming to see him. In all the years that he was at the nursing home Jim and I would go to see him and take him shopping and then to lunch.

Entry in Journal January 6 1994

Started the New Year as usual, took Jim to the doctor and he put him in the hospital. He had another

141

attack and couldn't breathe. Most of the time they would give him a breathing treatment and that helped so that he could come home. It was getting so that he was getting more attacks. This time he had pneumonia in his right lung and they put him on an I.V. The next day I found him walking around and complaining, which means that he was feeling better and he wanted to come home. I called Dr. Biddie's office, Nancy his nurse answered, I asked her to tell the doctor if Jim could come home tomorrow. The doctor said he couldn't leave until Thursday. The next day when I went to the hospital Jim wasn't happy because he had to stay another day. I came home that night and it was very windy and the TV Antenna wire came off the tower. Angela and Ray came over that night to put the treadmill together so that Jim could use it when he came home. Jim loved to walk and it was too cold to go outside in the winter so we bought the treadmill. I told Ray about the antenna but it was too late to fix it.

Entry in Journal January 7 1994

School called but I didn't go. I went to the hospital to take Jim home. It was a good day and it wasn't too cold. He has to take an antibiotic because his lung is not quite clear, its only 80% clear. He was happy to be home but he was kind of weak. The pills the doctor prescribed cost $66 for 10 pills.

We discussed getting cable which he doesn't want, but I explained that he can't go up the roof and I can't depend on anyone to go up there. I called to find out how much it would cost. *We did get cable.*

Jim was taking his medicine and was feeling a little better. He was using the treadmill and reading about his condition.

Entry in Journal January 14 1994

Yesterday was a snow day and I was glad to be home. I have a sinus infection and felt like I wanted to stay in bed all day. Jim was happy that I was home yesterday but he didn't want me to go to work today. I had Mrs. Ferrara's English class, one of my favorite classes and quite a few students were out because of the weather. It was still snowing and the periods were short because of the morning delay.

Our life took on a routine all winter, taking him under the care of the doctor and trying to get his condition stabilized. I can't wait till summer comes.

Entry in Journal Summer June 11 1994

He did little things around the house and that made him feel good. He wanted to do the lawns but that would affect his breathing, so I did the mowing, which I enjoyed doing.

Entry in Journal June 14 1994

Jim was a little better this weekend. It was almost the end of the school year and I was looking forward to the summer months and maybe Jim would feel better. My routine was going to be hectic, doing a lot of things that Jim would do. The lawns had to be mowed, his vegetable garden needed taken care, which he loved, which was something he so much wanted to have even though he couldn't take care of it. I would tell him that we had Story's Farm down the hill from our house, and we could get all the fresh produce we need. It made him happy to see things growing.

Then the summer people from the city would come up to see us. Ninety-four and very opinionated, Mrs. Davis was a spunky old lady and she was my mother's dearest friend, whom adopted me. She had a bungalow down the road from our house. Every summer since my mother had died it was a fact that I would take her shopping once a week when she was up for the summer. This year I wrote in my journal that I didn't want to take her shopping.

About Mrs. Davis, I didn't know how to tell her that I really didn't want to take her shopping. I wanted to be free of all commitments. Taking her shopping, she would spend two hours in the store and bought eighty nine dollars worth of food, and then we went to Story's Farm for vegetables. She was very grateful and said I am her extended family. She really should stay in the city, because it is getting too much for her to do. She really needs someone to do the cleaning and stay with her. The place needs painting, but she insisted that it's fine. When she was younger it was great to have her walk to our house and stay for tea, but now she can't walk that far so she keeps calling for me to keep her company. I should call her sons, and I can't take the responsibility for her well being. I guess I will do it the rest of summer and I am trying to take one day at a time. Jim is still the same.

Chapter Eighteen

September 1994

Jim's condition didn't change; he was still filled with fluid and wasn't eating very much. I cooked all summer and made the food that he loved. He's still under the doctor's care and isn't getting better. I know he's not happy about himself. He seems to love to give me all his troubles. I wish I could help him but he doesn't want to get any more help. He hates himself. Angela brought him some books on gadgets that can help him get his socks on. I didn't interfere with them as they went through the book's he wanted to do things for himself. He will probably want to make something for himself.

Day 4 into the New School Year

I really don't understand why but it made me feel alive to get back to school with the high school students. Maybe it brings back memories of when I was young and how much I loved school. *I really feel that it isn't easy for the students, with the entire curriculum that they have in today's world, plus other activities that they had time to put on a school play.*

Entry in Journal September 1994

I have two math classes; today so far the students are great. Mrs. Markle was in period 1 class to help the students one on one. We now have special education students in main stream classes and they need special attention. Some grasp the concept of the subject while others need help. I have been working quite a few days a week and Jim has been Ok for a while.

Had Another Problem

Had a problem at the Post office, I had called before I went and asked them to put my SS check aside so I could get it before the bank closed. This was the first time I had asked. I am the last person to get my mail for the day. When I arrived there Wendy was serving another patron. He also had a check with his mail which was on the counter. Wendy gave me my check and said to me that she would not give me my check if someone else was there. At this point I felt that there was another person who had his check and that if she had told him the same thing. I became angry and I told her so. She knew every body's business and I didn't trust her.

Entry in Journal Sept. 11 1994

Went to Catskill Saving Bank and made arrangements to Direct Deposit our checks. Hopefully it won't be too much trouble. I really like to see my checks and this way I know how much of a fixed balance I have. Oh well, wait and see.

We had always loved the winter months but now I knew that meant another year that Jim would get sick and he was too weak to fight another bout of Asthma or Pneumonia. He didn't go out in winter very often but he kept busy reading the medical books I brought home from the library. He wanted to get better and would say if he lived to be 100 years old he would always have something to do round the house.

Jim's Medals December 16 1994

Yesterday I picked up Jim's medals from the V. A. Bob Whitbeck also put in another claim for the rest of his war records and what he did during the war and he was very interested in helping us. When I started to find out about Jim's record in the Army I just knew he had something more coming to him. I am only sorry we didn't do it sooner. He had such an interesting life and he never realized how much he did in the war. My one wish for him now is that he would get better and enjoy the rest of his life. Only God knows what's in store for us. Tomorrow we have to go to Kingston to get fish for the holiday, and the fixings for the Italian cookies which I make only at Christmas time. I am glad that we are going to be all together again this year, for we don't know what the New Year will bring. I hope it will be good health for all the family

The Worst Year of My Life 1995 January

Another year and Jim isn't getting any better. The nights are always the same; he's up almost every night. I feel that something is going to happen. Monday night he threw up blood and that really scared me. His condition is critical and he needs to be in the hospital. I know that if I take him he will not make it, he hasn't the strength to fight it. I am always the one who insisted that he go. It is his decision to go to the hospital. He wasn't eating very much and was full of fluid. When I did take him that night to the hospital he had a hard time breathing and he wanted a treatment. The doctor in charge told me that he was going to die and the treatment was not going to help him. I thought that doctor had no right to tell me that. I answered, give him the treatment and I will pay for it. They did give him the treatment and he felt a little better.

Jim was still hanging on to life maybe just maybe he had a chance, he would make it. We got thru January going back and forth to the hospital for the treatment.

Jim Received the Rest of His Medals February 21 1995

We had asked Bob Whitbeck to put in another claim for his files of what he did in the war. In the process of finding some of his files, we discovered that he was supposed to have received two Bronze Stars and a host of other medals. On February 21, 1995, fifty years later his medals came thru the mail. It so happened that our grandson James, named after him was there to open the package with all his medals. Jim didn't have the strength to open the package. He was surprised that he had medals in his files. When he talked to me about the war and how many times he escaped being caught I would always ask, didn't someone write down what he had done. His answer was always the same, do you think that the people in charge had time during the war. *Evidently someone did.*

I saw a difference in him after he received his citations; he started to talk about the war and told his grandchildren how bad it was. He talked about his friends that were killed and one that had the same last name as his and that he was killed. One of his friends that he knew in boot camp came home with him after the war. In his account of all his duties as a RIFLEMAN, he was sent out alone to find where the enemy was. As a messenger he delivered verbal and written messages from Company to Battalion and Regiment.

148

NAME (Last, first, middle)	2 DEPARTMENT, COMPONENT AND BRANCH	3. SOCIAL SECURITY NO. (Also, Service Number if applicable)		
GULINO JAMES	ARMY AUS CMP			
MAILING ADDRESS (Include ZIP Code)				
132-15 75TH ST OZONE PARK NY		32	614	254

ORIGINAL ENTRIES CORRECTED AS INDICATED BELOW

ITEM NO.	WD AGO FORM 53-55	CORRECTED TO READ
	SEPARATION DATE ON DD FORM 214 BEING CORRECTED :	25 OCT 45

33	DELETE: EAME THEATER RIBBON ADD: EUROPEAN AFRICAN MIDDLE EASTERN CAMPAIGN MEDAL W/TWO BRONZE SERVICE STARS//BRONZE STAR MEDAL//GOOD CONDUCT MEDAL//MERITORIOUS UNIT EMBLEM//AMERICAN CAMPAIGN MEDAL//WW II VICTORY MEDAL//NOTHING FOLLOWS

DATE	7. TYPED NAME, GRADE, TITLE AND SIGNATURE OF OFFICIAL AUTHORIZED TO SIGN
28 MARCH 1994	ROSE M BROWN GS-8 CHIEF VSE-A ABERDEEN

DD FORM 215
JUL 79

PREVIOUS EDITIONS
OF THIS FORM ARE
OBSOLETE.

CORRECTION TO DD FORM 214, CERTIFICATE OF RELEASE OR DISCHARGE FROM ACTIVE DUTY

MEMBER 1

SUMMARY OF MILITARY OCCUPATIONS

13. TITLE—DESCRIPTION—RELATED CIVILIAN OCCUPATION

RIFLEMAN -- In U.S., France, Belgium, Holland and Germany, fired M1 rifle, carbine, Browning automatic rifle, and light machine gun. Disassembled, cleaned and reassembled weapons.

As messenger delivered verbal and written messages from Company to Battalion and Regiment. RELATED CIVILIAN OCCUPATION -- Assembler.

WD AGO FORM 100
1 FEB 1945

This form supersedes WD AGO Form 100, 15 July 1944, which will not be used.

149

Our 50ᵗʰ Anniversary April 8 1995

We had planned to celebrate and take our children and grandchildren to a family dinner but our plans had to change. Jim was too sick and we couldn't take him out. He was so depressed that our plans had to change so children and grandchildren would celebrate at home. They planned to have a small gathering with them and our close friends. We thought that we would serve Jim's favorite food which he didn't have in such a long time, Fried Chicken. Our granddaughter Maria Elena made a beautiful anniversary cake and Grandpa Jim really enjoyed that. It didn't matter what he ate anymore because it wouldn't change what would happen, I felt that we were blessed to reach our 50ᵗʰ anniversary and now maybe we would have a little miracle but, this never happened.

The Morning of May 3 1995

I was up early that morning. Jim woke up at seven thirty and I helped him get to the bathroom. I asked if he wanted to have breakfast with me; I would make whatever he wanted, he said he was tired and wanted to go back to sleep. I went into the kitchen and had breakfast, a soft boiled egg with tea and toast. I had left the door opened to the bedroom a little so that I could look in and see if he was alright. I found that his legs were half way out of the bed, I went in to help him but that was when I realized that he was gone. I didn't panic, I closed his eyes and put his legs on the bed and covered him. I called my son in law Joe, my daughter Nancy's husband and told him to come over. I don't remember too much about the funeral except that Jim never wanted to wear a suit so I told them to put him in his favorite sweats and his moccasins. We only had a simple funeral Jim didn't like funerals and also hated to go to one. My two Grandsons folded the flag that was on his casket, and I still have it.

I didn't cry because I had cried for four years by myself and now he was at peace and wouldn't suffer anymore. He put on a good fight and I am glad I was home with him.

Now most of all I remember the four years that Jim went through and all the suffering he tolerated. 1994 was his worst year which he spent going back and forth to the hospital for treatments. We never talked about his condition and that there was no hope that he would get better, we lived one day at a time. Most of the time he would read about his condition and I would get new information from the computer in the school library, and hope that maybe they had a new procedure for his condition and it would help.

What made Jim depressed was that he needed help with his personal needs. He couldn't shower by himself, I cut his hair did his nails and shaved him. He had lost a lot of weight and was skin and bones. His stomach was swollen to a degree that his waist was fifty inches and his feet were double their size. *His famous words were "how can you look at me in this condition". "I love you and you will be my soul mate for the rest of my life and I'll never give up."*

Chapter Nineteen

My Life After Jim's Death

1996

I really didn't know what to do first. So I decided that I would go back to school to get my B.A.

This was going to be a problem; I had to keep working as a Sub and I could only go back in the afternoon after school was out. One of the teachers's suggested that Empire State College had an instructor at our Columbia Greene Community College which was available near our town.

When I first applied for the course, the time period was set for three to four in the afternoon. I was also told that I was to write a paper on (Academic Planning), this had three sections Topics, Learning Activities, and Evaluation. Every time I went to meet the instructor she was always in a hurry to leave, and I felt that she didn't want me as a student. This wasn't going to work out well. When I first handed in my paper of thirteen pages with the three sections, I was told that it wasn't good enough. She didn't have the courtesy to tell me what was wrong with the paper and just put the paper in her desk drawer.

This was very discouraging so I didn't finish this course. I didn't give up though; at the time I left, there were more pressing things that I had to do. My feeling of being alone was impossible to describe. How was I going to survive? How could I take care of all the things that Jim did? The lawns needed to be mowed, the changing of the light bulbs in the house, getting a new roof on the house, which was badly needed. Jim had said we couldn't do it because he wanted help to put it on. The more I thought about what had to be done I realized that it was a challenge and it now was my responsibility. Where do I start first? There was so much to do and not enough money. I was seventy one; the only thing that helped me was the fact that I was still working as a Sub Teacher, so that would supplement my income.

Just before Jim passed we had put another claim in for his pension. This time I received a letter from the Veterans Administration stating that they had lost his files and therefore they couldn't process his claim.

Empire State College February 1996

I called the office of Empire State College and they made arrangements for me to meet two other instructors. I had to go to Albany to see them and that meant I had to drive forty miles each ways. I was determined to get on with my education, so I went. The interview went well and I signed a learning contract. I was taking two courses; one was Education Psychology with instructor Barg, four credits and Developing Written a Voice by Dona J Hickey with instructor William, another four credits. I accomplished the courses and received my eight credits, the hard way, with my working and traveling to Albany. I didn't continue with Empire State College because I discovered that I felt the need of a different learning experience.

Wrote a Letter to the President 1996

Well, I thought...what would happen if I wrote a letter to President Clinton and explained my problem? I figured that, "What did I have to lose, another rejection or would it be a waste of time?" So, I mailed the letter.

HC1 715 Stony Brook Ext.
Palenville, NY 12463

April 3, 1996

File Number:
James Gulino

President Clinton
c/o Office of Presidential Correspondence
White House
Washington, DC 20500

Dear Mr. President:

The reason I am writing this letter is that I believe my problem should be addressed.

I met James Gulino in 1941. At the time he was working and in perfect health. He was inducted in 1942 and was in the Army until 1945. When in the Army he went through vigorous maneuvers and still was fine. He was in the 413th Timberwolf Division of the 104th Infantry. His assignment in the Army was a messenger. He served his unit very well including reporting back to his unit the position of his enemy. He also captured several enemy soldiers. What is ironic is that he never knew he was the recipient of the Bronze Star and all his other medals until 1994. This came about when we applied for his records and disability in 1994. He was critically ill at the time.

His medals came February 21, 1995, 2 months before he passed away on May 3, 1995. It is also ironic that particular week he passed away was the 50th anniversary of the end of World War II. We also celebrated our 50th wedding anniversary on April 8 (1945-1995). It really made a difference in his last days after being in poor health most of his life.

At this point in time his disability case is still pending. After the government furlough the Department of Veterans Affairs, 245 W. Houston Street, New York, NY 10014, lost his files. His file number is

Mr. Robert B. Whithbeck, Director of Veterans Service of Catskill, NY 12414, has been in touch with the Department of Veterans Affairs every week since the government's return to work. And they have not yet found the files.

44

To my surprise I received an answer from when I sent the letter in April of 96th to May of 96th when I received the letter from the White House stating to get in touch with the Veterans Administration in Catskill and request a hearing of his case.

THE WHITE HOUSE
WASHINGTON

May 8, 1996

Mrs. James Gulino
Route 1, 715 Stony Brook Extension
Palenville, New York 12463

Dear Mrs. Gulino:

Thank you so much for your letter. President Clinton greatly appreciates the trust and confidence you have shown in him by writing.

To ensure that your concerns are addressed, I am forwarding your letter to the Department of Veterans Affairs for review and any appropriate action. Please bear in mind that it may take some time to look thoroughly into the issues you have raised. Should you wish to contact the Department of Veterans Affairs directly, you may write to: Department of Veterans Affairs, 810 Vermont Avenue, N.W., Washington, D.C. 20420.

Many thanks for your patience.

Sincerely,

James A. Dorskind
Special Assistant to the President
Director of Correspondence and
Presidential Messages

I called Director Robert B. Whitbeck of the Veterans Service Agency of Catskill N.Y. whom was in charge of Jim's case and he felt that we needed more information about Jim's life.

This time I didn't take it lightly and decided that I would finish his portfolio and present it at the hearing. With the help of Bob and Mary, his secretary who called and got a hearing in September of '96 and also had Representative Dan Morea of the America Legion present at the hearing.

INDEX

158

56 Veterans Administration Regional Office NY:June 1972 In
                        hospital May 17 to June 23 1972

59 Department of Health Education and Welfare-Social
   Security Administration
   General Authorization for Medical Information
67 Bureau of Disability Determination

75 Social Security Award Certificate:Disability

77 American Bakery and Confectionery Workers Union Welfare
                                              Fund
80 Department of Veterans Affairs:Samuel S Stratton Medical
   Center Albany NY May 28-June 7 1976 January 25-27 1990

83 Columbia Greene Medical Center Catskill NY:Medical
                                             Records
84 Kingston Hospital:Medical Records 2/25/93 to 4/7/93

94 Kingston Hospital:Medical Records 1/6/94 to 1/13/94

99 Some Medications taken over most of his Life some others
                        taken off the market.

109 Request of Medical Record from Department of Medical
                    Center NY Reply-1996-1994

111 Rating Decisions:10/30/45 6/5/72 9/19/95 3/7/96 4/16/96
                              5/13/96 5/23/96

117 Appeal:Statement of Case July 1 1996

118 Earnings of James from 1950-1975

119-Earnings of Tina 1944-1996

The Hearing September 1996

Not having been into New York City in quite a few years and of course, I wouldn't drive to the city. My daughter Angela and I took the Amtrak train in Hudson that took us to the city. I was now prepared with Jim's portfolio in hand and with 110 pages of his life from when he was 16 years old until his death. I didn't care anymore if they only would give me a yes or no answer. Being what I had gone through at this time in life I could cope with anything.

The hearing went well and the Hearing Officer in charge asked for a favor. He wanted me to leave the portfolio so that he could look at it. My answer was yes, under one condition, that I wanted it back because it belonged to my children, they were very proud of him.

Subject: Letter of Thank You and Appreciation

Date: December 1996

Dear Mr. Whitbeck,

A simple Thank You is always so formal. To tell a person how you feel inside is so hard to express, but I will try.

Bob, when we started this venture with the Veteran's Administration the outcome seemed fruitless. It took from March 1994 to September 1996 to accomplish the undertaking with the VA.

I always felt that our claim was justified. After fifty years of my husband's condition it is unbelievable that a Medical Corp.person decided not to grant my husband a disability discharge from Rhoads General Hospital.

Also in 1994 you sent a request to the US Army Reserve Personnel Center for any Awards that Jim had received during World War 2. It was ironic that he received his Bronze Star Medal and other awards on February 21, 1995, fifty years later. These awards came at a most important time in his life. He was critically ill and to know what he did made a difference to our family. Jim passed away on May 3, 1995.

This wasn't all that you help me with. Applying for Death Indemnity Compensation(DIC), which also was rejected for the same reasons as before, (not service connected). You felt that we needed more proof and asked if I had any.

I gathered all personal papers, letters and pictures from the day I met Jim in 1941, complied a portfolio. This was presented at a hearing in the Veteran's Administration Building in New York City, with Dan Morea , representative from the America Legion. This time it worked.

There were times when claim after claim was denied, but you were always there with another idea and another form. You, Dan and Mary we were a team. Bob, you were instrumental in giving my life order and direction at a time when it seemed so discouraging. Through this venture the most important thing happened to us, our friendships.

Yours truly,

Vinny Died July 1997

No sooner that I finished my courses at Empire State College I had another issue to take care of, Jim's brother Vinny whom was in a nursing home passed away. I remembered when Jim's father died in 1963; the burden was ours, there were decisions to make then. Who was going to take care of him? We had a meeting with his brother and his sister who lived only a block away but couldn't go over and help him. The conclusion was that Vinny could stay in the apartment and Jim and Sal would go over Saturday to take him shopping and help him clean the apartment. Sal lived in Long Island and most of the time he couldn't come into Brooklyn. Eventually that left Jim and I to take care of him.

Not to have Vinny living with us, Jim and I felt he wouldn't be a stable person to have around our daughters. He would sometimes get drunk; this went on for sixteen years, until he didn't take care of his personal stuff. We all decided to put him in an assisted living facility. He wasn't there too long because we were moving upstate and had to find another facility for him. We moved in 1986 and put Vinny in Long Term Care in Catskill, NY. Our daughter Angela lived up there and was a nurse in that facility so she kept an eye on him. It was only eight miles away from our house so every time we went to town we would go see Vinny. He loved going to Dunkin Donuts for coffee and donuts and took him shopping for some of his needs.

When Jim's brother Vinny passed away at age 83 and out lived my husband who passed in1995 it was my duty to send the body downstate to be buried with his father in St John's Cemetery. I thought that this was another stressful time in my life.

Chapter Twenty

My World Came Tumbling Down

May 1998

This was the year when my world came tumbling down. I thought now I could relax and maybe I can go back to college or go to see my brother in Florida, but I was wrong. I was going to be tested with so many more problems and decisions that only I had to make. Knowing that I had a Cystic breast at age 35 it was a habit for me to always examine them when I took my shower.

In May of that year in a routine examination of my breast I felt a small pea lump in one of them. It was in my left breast. I called my primary doctor and he recommended a doctor that was a specialist at Benedictine Hospital in Kingston. I called for an appointment to see Dr. Sheldon Feldman. I received a date in the middle of May. I often wonder how I was going to feel when I found a lump.

Well, I didn't say "WHY ME?" All I wanted was get this thing out as soon as possible. Not knowing if it was cancer or how bad it was, had it spread to my lymph nodes. Was I going to have chemo or radiation, or could I have a lumpectomy?

My father had lung Cancer and they gave him Chemo and then his blood turned to water or that it burned his body. I always felt that they gave him too much Chemo and weakened his immune symptom. Maybe he would have lived longer if he didn't get so much medication. *They now monitor how much Chemo they give to cancer patients.*

Getting back to Dr. Feldman, when I first met him I wondered how young he was to take on such a devastating problem. I soon found out that he was the founder of the Feldman Breast Cancer Center at Benedictine hospital in his sister's name. She was very young when she passed away. This inspired him to devote his time to research and causes of breast cancer. I went with my daughter Angela who is an R.N. He explained some of the procedures. He first wanted a biopsy, this would give him an idea if the small pea was cancer or not. I remembered watching the screen as he probed my breast. It didn't hurt and he was so gentle but also sympathetic for all the women and they, in turn felt that he was there for them in the scariest time of their life. The doctor didn't get the results of the biopsy until a week later, it was cancer. He said that my cancer was only a 1.5 and it was in a capsule and had not invaded my lymph nodes.

Now there were decisions I had to make. I asked my daughter Angela, the nurse what should I do, her answer was, Mom I can't make that decision, it's your body and only you know what you want. What I felt was that Jim had passed away so maybe instead of a lumpectomy which meant that I would have to get Chemo and Radiation. Removing the whole breast I would have a better chance that the Cancer may never come back again. So I decided to have the Mastectomy. To lose a breast and to be deformed, well the problem was I wanted the Cancer out of my body and take my chances that I made the right decision. I would be fine and everything was set. The operation was scheduled for June 1st.

What happened next was something I never expected. On May 23 I was going to have a garage sale to get rid of some clutter. I spent most of the day getting ready for the sale and after a while I felt kind of sick. I had cramps in my stomach, so I lay down but felt warm, I took my temperature it was 102. I knew that something was wrong because I hardly ever get a fever. I called my daughter whom was at her daughter's house and she told me to lie on bed and bring my knee up to my chest, "Are you kidding?" I said, it hurt too much. Anyway she told me to call Nancy my other daughter to take me to the hospital right away. Of course I said, I'll wait till you come home. Her reply was I'll meet you there. She also called her sister to make sure that Nancy was taking me to the hospital. At this point I knew that Angela was serious. She was right, at the hospital they took a Cat-Scan and sure enough my appendix had ruptured, I was operated at 12 o'clock midnight. This was the worst six days I ever experienced. First of all I was on an I. V. and antibiotics for six days and no food. During the night and day I had to relieve myself, every hour on the hour with the medication on the stand. The nurses were busy with more critical patients. On the 6th day I felt I had lost control of my body and wanted to get out of there. The night before they had given me something to help me sleep, I didn't sleep, they had given me the drug Demerol and the reaction to it was that I saw spiders on the wall. In the morning my doctor came in to make rounds and saw that I was upset and crying, I told him what I saw and he proceeded to remove the I.V. and ordered a chicken salad sandwich. No way, all I wanted was a cup of tea and some crackers. It worked and I went home the next day.

My problems were not over yet. I had to deal with the breast operation. I was in no mood to go back to the hospital, but I knew that my cancer would have to be dealt with.

On July 1st I went in for a radical mastectomy. As much as it was a big operation I told the doctor that I didn't want to stay in the hospital. I went home the next day with a drain attached and they showed me how to measure the fluids. My daughter, the nurse came in and took my temperature before she went to work. After ten days the drain was taken out and I was fine. This operation was more radical than the appendectomy but knowing that part of my body was taken off I could accept it. The cancer was gone. I felt that now I could get on with my life. I refused chemo and radiation from the oncologist and he became upset with me and his bedside manner left me with the impression that I wouldn't want him for my doctor. I told him it was my body and that I took the breast off so that I would not take Chemo or Radiation. When I went back to my Cancer doctor I asked Dr. Feldman a question, how long have I got? Five years? He said he didn't know, but with my attitude I would be fine. I told him that I was thinking about going back to college and get my B.A.

School Trip to Spain April 1999

After being home the rest of the summer, come September, I went back to work at the school. I was glad to finally get my health back. I really had to prove that I was going to be fine. It was great to see everyone at school, the only thing that hadn't changed was that we had a new principal. *Our school, in the nineteen years that I was there we had changed about fifteen administrators and each one had their own way of running the school.* This principal, I'll call Mr. B was a Lieutenant in the Army and believed that he would run the school with the rules of the Army. I really felt that I needed more time for myself.

Well, as it so happen Mr. T McKay, the head of the Spanish department, was planning a trip to Spain and they needed some adults to chaperone the fifteen students. I felt that I would be happy to go, and not be subbing every day. Maybe I didn't have the patience to handle another administration. Most of the time I had subbed for Donna Wheat, one of the Spanish teachers and I volunteered to go, but I did pay for my trip. *Jim and I had traveled to Europe but we never went to Spain,* so I joined the group. It was a very interesting trip and we went to the northern part of Spain, Toledo, Salamanca, Segovia, and Madrid; most of the time we were in charge of the students. Mary Hatton and Danna Wheat knew every part of Spain, Donna had gone to school there. We seen quite a few castles and cathedrals and almost everything were made in gold, even the caskets of the dead royalists were of it. *In Italy, almost everything was made of marble and gold leaf.*

Our Castle in Disney World is a replica of one of the Castles in Spain, so the saying goes.

There was one incident that I must tell you. In one of the hotels where we went for dinner, the main course was fish. In Europe fish is served with the head on. Well when the fish was served, fifteen students almost passed out. How could they eat a fish with a head and eye staring at them? I must admit that even the teachers weren't too pleased with the fish. I of course was used to

169

eating fish that way so it didn't faze me; all eyes were on me to see how to tackle the fish. The student's refused to eat the fish so they had to get them something else to eat. Most of the teachers tackled the fish after they saw what I did. *After fishing with my Father and Mom cooking fish, it came in handy as how to eat a whole fish.*

Another exciting incident was on the way back home. Our flight was canceled and our group was separated into different flights, this of course alarmed the students, most had phoned their parents to pick them up. This caused more trouble for us; we had to divide the students so that some of the adult's went with other students on another flight. The students were afraid and wanted their friends with them. We tried reassuring the students that everything would be fine, and they would get home a little late. The flights were not going to take off at the same time, so we had to take the students that were frightened first. I really don't remember which went first but I do remember that I was on the last flight to Albany. I do remember that my daughter Nancy and Joe waited until 2:30 in the morning when my plane landed. It was quite an adventure, and that was the last trip to Europe.

When we finally got back from Spain, at two-o-clock in the morning I really was too tired to go back to work. The following week when I went back, things hadn't changed and this was when I really told myself that I would go back to college. I needed time for myself and I didn't want to put up with his changes. There was also conflict with Karin whom was the principal of the Middle School. She had made many changes in the school and did a fantastic job in the Middle School. Mr. B didn't want to listen to anyone. I recall him saying that I was doing a good job as a substitute teacher, but that he believed that in his mind I was getting too old to be a teacher. There were many days that I didn't enjoy going to work, there were always different rules and he insisted we use Army jargon in communicating with him. I knew it was time for me to make my decision now and to give myself some space from working almost every day at the school.

Chapter Twenty One

Another Challenge

Enrolled at University of New Paltz

2000

This time, going to college wasn't going to be easy; traveling forty miles from my house to New Paltz and then back forty miles. Of all times to start College, in the dead of winter and I knew what my heart said, but didn't realize what I was in for. My age and what I had gone through, could I do it? I still felt that I could do it.

So, in the beginning of January 2000 I had sent for all the paper work and applied at the University of New Paltz, there I met with Mike Husenits the Coordinator for transfer admissions and we went over my papers. We decided that my major would be Communication and Media.

January 2000 my first semester, I took two classes, the first was Persuasion and the second was Introduction to Interpersonal Communication. My first instructor of the class of Persuasion, she gave an assignment but didn't really give much explanation as to the specifics of it and most of the time the class was taught by a substitute. This made me feel as if I was a bad student and what was I thinking going back to college that I can't understand what is going on? In this class, I received a D, in all my educational endeavors this was the first time that this had ever happened and I began to question myself as a person, "how bad was I?" Maybe I was getting too old to learn something new? Do I really want to travel 80 miles each way for this?

When I went to Mike Lecesses's class, I told him that I was going to quit. He was quite upset with me and told me to "stick it out" and not to let one instructor determine my decision.

I took Mike L's advice and didn't quit. As time went on, I remember how I got into the routine of Mike's classes. One assignment, which I distinctly remember, I was paired with a 20 year old student named Jeff. Our assignment was that we should pretend that we were going to get married. He and I had to travel to a jewelry store to buy a wedding band. So, I said to Mike... I don't know, I don't think that this is going to work, but we decided to do the assignment anyway. Jeff and I decided to go to JC Penney's. There were two other students that were assigned to this project to witness us as we shopped. Well, to our surprise, when Jeff asked to see the rings, it did not phase the salesperson at all. She was only interested in making the sale. We also went to another jewelry store and the same scene played out as well. Jeff and I couldn't believe that the sales people didn't look at the differences in our ages. In the next class, we presented our findings; our witnesses' agreed that the salesperson didn't think about our ages. Mike always made his classes interesting and assigning outlandish assignments. I went on to take on many classes, most of the instructors were great; however, Mike and Marie Lecesse stand out because they were pivotal in my decision to stay in. I am forever grateful to them.

Another class that truly comes to mind was "Non-verbal Communication". Here is an excerpt of the paper that I wrote for that class. It is entitled "Reflection." Being in a Summer Session in college, I have a limited amount of time on the weekend. I had told my family that I had to finish two papers for both of my classes.

Most of the time my daughters came over on Sunday morning and would bring me the newspaper; they understood the situation and would leave the paper in between the door and the house.

I knew that this day was going to be hectic. I had it all planned exactly how my day was going to be; I would finish the assigned papers and maybe I could go shopping later in the day. Well, it didn't happen that way at all. Typing away on the computer, the doorbell rang. Leaving my computer in the middle of the paper, I answered the door. It was my very best friend Jo whom I haven't seen since the beginning of June. She is a mentor for one of my students from Catskill high school. Surprised to see her, I stood by the door, and said in a non-verbal gesture... "What are you doing here?" She must have noticed the blank expression on my face, because she apologized for just coming over without calling first. I was glad to see her, but explained that I was pressed for time. She said that she was in the neighborhood and just wanted to say hello.

How could I make this bad situation better? So, I said, let's sit outside on the swing. I offered her some ice cream and we sat eating and reminiscing. I then started to clean up the dishes as a non-verbal cue that I needed to get back to writing. Jo and I have been friends for over fourteen years and we truly rely on our non-verbal communication. She understood about my needing time to finish my paper.

Another example of non-verbal communication that sticks in my mind that I recall was also with my husband in regards to my children. When the girls wanted to go out and I didn't approve of where they were going, I would say to them, "Ask your father". When they asked him, he would look at me and I would just roll my eyes and he would read the expression on my face. *This worked perfectly until they got older and became aware of our signals.*

Graduation December 15 2001

I really couldn't believe that I made it. I had so many people saying, *why didn't you retire. It was a dream that I had when I had to leave school at sixteen.*

At this point, I want to go onto a tangent and mention someone very important to me, who knew how important it was for me to get my B.A. We have been friends for over 40 years and she has done my hair for most of the important times of my life and this was one of the times she wanted to be part of it. Do I have any secrets? *Only my hairdresser would know.*

In 1967, when Jim and I first bought our house in Upstate NY, on the way back to the city, I would stop and get my hair washed and set. She has become part of my life and vice versa as well as that of my children. Many times she shared with me our ups and downs. One thing about Teri, my family could tell her anything and you would know that your secret is safe with her forever. We have had many a talk about health, religion, politics, emotions, and every conceivable subject. Sometimes we disagreed on a subject but we always discussed the other's point of view and sometimes could convince the other person to change their mind. In the 42 years it's always been a joy to visit her little shop in the back of her garage. For me, it is called "emotional therapy" to go once a week to have my hair done and she always knows how I like it done. I always come out refreshed and emotionally content.

Entry in Journal 2001

Was it really worth going 80 miles a day and going thru the winter sessions at the college? Yes! In the winter I would follow the snow plow on the way home at night on the Thruway, a main road that lead to the college. I kept reminding myself of my goal and that I really did it.

The biggest surprise was when the bell rang at my house and my baby brother Frankie, was there. He had driven up from Florida to be at my graduation. He also was the one that told a reporter from "The Freeman", that I was one of the oldest students graduating that year. Enclosed is the news article, published by "The Freeman" under the title, "She's the class of '01"written: By Paula Ann Mitchell, correspondent. I also appeared on WTBY-TV54 Trinity Broadcasting of New York. January 27, 2002 was my fifteen minutes of fame.

After graduation, I went back to work. Our superintendent, Dr. G. Wolf offered me a job in the elementary school. I refused and I felt that I wanted to stay at the high school as a substitute teacher. She was quite proud of me and asked me to come to one of the board meetings to honor my accomplishment of earning my bachelor's degree at the age of 77. I was caught by surprise by this and she also asked me to say a few words. I didn't really know what to say, all that came to mind was. *"It Is Never Too Late.*

She's the class of '01

By PAULA ANN MITCHELL, Correspondent   January 27, 2002

Tina Gulino of Palenville is proof that learning is a lifelong process. At 77, she did something few her age could match - she graduated from the State University of New York at New Paltz with a bachelor's degree in media communications.

Tina Gulino

The day was Dec. 15, 2001. Family and friends had gathered for the momentous occasion. In her cap and gown, the 5-foot-1-inch Gulino stood out from among the other fresh faces waiting to receive their degrees. Finally, her name was called.

She walked toward her dream and grasped it, she said, because her moment had arrived.

"It was a lifelong dream. It was something I had always wanted to do. I had done all the things for my family - my mother, my father, my brother, my husband, my children. Now it was my turn to do what I pleased, and I did it. It's never too late."

Gulino maintained a B average while attending the university, her mind always eager to absorb more material. Taking exams, however, was not her strength.

"I'm a very bad test-taker. I go blank, yet I can talk my way out of anything."

Not even the computer intimidated Gulino. Her grandchildren were her greatest supporters, though not everyone boosted her confidence.

178

"Some of my friends used to say, 'Learn the computer? What are you? Crazy?'

She said the computer "took me a while, but I began to love it. I did a lot of research on it for my papers. I'm thinking of taking an advanced computer class. There's so much to learn today."

It's that kind of enthusiasm that has carried her forward, observed Michael Lecesse, who teaches interpersonal communication at the college:

"I was very impressed with her. To have someone in her 70s in your class - that's a little special. She has a good common sense approach to life, and that only comes with age."

Lecesse, who became Gulino's mentor, said that's not always the case with older students.

"I get very leery of older students in my class because a lot of them feel they have something to prove," he said. "Tina is not like that. She's all around a really good person. I wish I had a class entirely of Tinas. It would make teaching so much easier."

Gulino is extraordinary not just because of her age, but because she never missed a class. Not even last winter's fury could keep her away, and her commute was an 80-mile drive each day.

'I never played hooky, even last winter. I had a lot of afternoon classes, and the roads were pretty clear by then," she said.

When she had no scheduled classes, Gulino worked as a substitute teacher at Catskill High School, something she's been doing for 14 years.

"When I got home every day, I had homework. It was hard, but I did it."

Her determination stems in part from her past. At 16, she was forced to leave school to care for her baby brother during the Great Depression.

"There were five children, and I was the oldest. My dad was a mailman ... and my mother was a full-time seamstress. I had to quit school for two years, and then I went to work in the garment industry."

After a series of jobs, Gulino became production manager at J. Heckler & Co. in Brooklyn. She then ran a dress shop from 1976 to 1978, all the while caring for a family, including her husband, James, and two daughters. Though kin was always first for this proud Sicilian-American, something was missing.

She wanted to bring closure to the educational lapse in her life, never knowing that her next job would bring her back into the classroom.

She applied for work at Franklin K. Lane High School in Woodhaven and was hired in food services. Her union offered members a chance to pursue their degrees, so she attended evening classes at LaGuardia Community College where she earned an associate's degree in food service management. She made the dean's list twice and graduated in 1984.

Still not fulfilled, she took additional courses at Columbia-Greene Community College after her family moved from Ozone Park to Columbia County.

Meanwhile, she continued to care for James, who was in poor health. He died in May 1995, a month after their 50th wedding anniversary.

That wasn't the end of her difficulties. In 1998, she was diagnosed with breast cancer and opted for a mastectomy instead of chemotherapy treatments.

'After my operation, it was touch-and-go. I asked my doctor, 'How long do I have?' He said I had another 10 years or so. I thought, 'Before I die, I want to do something for me.'"

That's when she enrolled at SUNY New Paltz. Not long after, she met Jennifer Morris of Rhinebeck, another nontraditional student in her late 30s. The two became study buddies, often meeting at the popular New Paltz spot Jazzman's Cafe.

"We used to meet there for lunch and go over our notes and help each other," said Morris, who graduated with Gulino in December.

Morris said age was not a factor for Gulino: "It was as if there wasn't an age difference. She fit in very well. She brought a lot to the class - wisdom and knowledge. She was very well liked by the faculty, too."

On graduation day, Morris was as happy for Gulino as she was for herself.

'I was very proud of her," Morris said. "Between the two of us, we did what we set out to do. She has a lot of courage. I think it takes tremendous courage to go back (to school) at 77 and get your bachelor's degree."

Gulino's daughter, Angela Heyman of Palenville, echoes that sentiment:

"It was a thrill," Heyman said. "We were so proud of her. She's always been a believer in education. Schooling was very important to her.

"She has passed that on to us, to believe in ourselves and to keep going. She used to say, 'Whatever your goals are, you can reach them.' We're just really blessed to have her. Not many people can say they have a 77-year-old mother who graduated from college."

Even the brother she had once cared for, Frank, drove from Florida to watch her graduate. The family showered her with roses, took her to dinner and gave her a party.

Gulino now plans to do post-graduate work. She has no intention of getting a job in the field of communications: "If I go in and ask for a job, who's going to hire me? This wasn't something I did to make more money. It was something I needed."

Gulino credits much of her success to the support of family and friends. Keeping company with the teens at Catskill High School also has kept her mind sharp: "They make me feel young. I've always been around them. I love them."

180

Chapter Twenty Two

When My Life Changed

December 3 2003

The whole year of 2002 and most of 2003 went well; I was working almost every day. In September of the new term of 2003, when we received a new principal, I will call him Mr. Fille. He started just like all new administrators; they have to prove that they were in command. He was the one that told me that after eight years of parking in the front of the school building, now I had to park in the back of the building. Not to argue with him, I decided the first day to do it. In all the years that I had worked at the school, I reported to the office which was in the front entrance. Not familiar with the back of the building, and with the sun shining in my eyes, as I was leaving for the day, I didn't see the curb, I fell and hit a brick wall and hurt my neck, shoulder, tail bone and other parts on my right side. I lay there for 20 minutes, there was a young man that was one of my students that stood with me, after this time, I barely got up and somehow made it home. I really don't recall how I did it. The next morning my son-in-law took me to the hospital; they took x-rays and it showed multiple severe contusions of my neck, shoulder and tail bone which could not be fixed. My right arm was so bad that I couldn't wash my face nor comb my hair. The x-rays didn't show that my C-6 disk in my neck was hitting the spinal cord; it was shaped like an hourglass. My only concern was my health, would I ever get back to my normal self. The mornings were the worst time of the day; the pains in my arms and shoulder were stiff. I would mentally tell myself, I can do this.

Entry in Journal March 2004

I was home and under doctor's care for three months while receiving worker's compensation. I was put on Physical Therapy for my arm and shoulder and had a limited amount of uses. I went back to work in March not realizing that I wasn't feeling well; it seemed that I never felt the same after the fall and I became always afraid of falling down. This was the beginning of feeling that I would never be normal again.

I really didn't know for sure about an operation and going back to work and my life and if I could work. Knowing that if I couldn't work at doing what I loved, I would become depressed. Being home for seven weeks, re- enforced that feeling of depression. It made me realize that helping children, that I gave them stability and assurance that I also needed.

I went to three doctors and after many x-rays and MRIs they discovered that one of my discs, a C-6 cervical disk was protruding into my spine cord which gave me pain in both my arms and hands. I was told that any future fall would leave me paralyzed from the waist up if I didn't receive the operation. Dr. Richard Perkin's, the first doctor that had worked with me, had discovered what was wrong. My first thought was at 80 years old, what were my chances that I would survive coming out of this operation, this started a chain reaction. I was too afraid to go through the operation that he recommended, so I went to see a Specialist in Albany for a second opinion. Of course this had to first be approved by the Compensation doctor one of the doctors from the board was the one that said I was *"Tipsy"* because I had a weakness when I got off the examining table. I think that he could have used a more medical term for his observation, instead of using a term that normally is used to describe someone that is under the influence of alcohol. I do not drink because I am allergic to it, so I was a bit put off to say the least by his comment. Resenting the word and when I went to see Dr. Perkins, I expressed my opinion of what I thought the Comp. doctor wrote of my condition. My doctor laughed and said, he used quotes about the word. *I still think he could have used a medical term, in referring about my condition but maybe my life has been rather unsteady.*

In the meantime my life became a scarier mess, emotionally. What if I fell again and became paralyzed? I was put on compensation. I hated what happened to me and I was at the mercy of the comp. board. When will they approve the operation?

The Break-In May 20 2004

Since all the trouble I had after Jim's death, the ruptured appendix, breast cancer, the fall, did I need to go through another test. I didn't question what had happened before but this time I really questioned (WHY ME?). They say that when something happens and you get another problem, it makes you stronger.

I started worrying about what was going to happen next, but then something happened that took place that was scarier. On May 20th some memories in my life stand out in my subconscious and this one I'll never forget.

The morning started out like any other working day. I had a class on that day and also had a 3:00 appointment with one of my doctors at the end of the day's work, so I went straight from school to Kingston and didn't stop at home.

The rest of the incident is in a deposition that Investigator Tor O. Tryland of the Green County Sheriff's Office wrote, of what happened.

SUPPORTING DEPOSITION

GREENE COUNTY SHERIFF'S OFFICE

SEC 100.20 CPL

STATE OF NEW YORK
COUNTY OF GREENE
TOWN OF CATSKILL

On 05.20.2004 at 08:50 P..M. I, Tina Gulino, DOB: 03.19.24 of 11 Stony Brook Ext. Palenville NY. Phone # 678-9735.

NOTE: This statement will be in a Question / Answer format. Q: Denotes a question asked by Inv. Tryland, and A: Denotes an answer given by Tina Gulino.

STATE THE FOLLOWING :
Q: An incident took place at your residence on Stony Brook Ext. today, tell me what happened?
A: At 6:30 I came home from Kingston, on route 31, and as I took the stuff from my car I noticed that a windsock was on the ground. I thought nothing of it and walked inside. As I got inside I noticed hairspray, wipes and my go-away bag on the floor, and then I turned the TV on. I took a TV dinner from the refrigerator and put it into the micro wave. After this I was taking off my blouse as I was going into my bedroom. As I get into the bedroom I saw a male person onmy bed. For a minute I thought it was my grandson Thomas, and I went to touch him to wake him up.
Q: Then what happened?
A: As I got close enough to touch him, I touched his right shoulder to wake him. As I was doing this I noticed that the person had a tattoo on his upper right arm, so it was not my grandson.
Q: Can you describe the tattoo?
A: It was a funny looking thing, I didn't get the whole picture, it had a bluish color, and I would have to describe it as a the bottom part of a Chinese design.
Q: Then what happened?
A: He was stirred, but not awake, and I decided that I had to get out before he could hurt me. I went outside, and I locked the door as I left. I tried to use the phone in the garage, but I was not able to dial the number, so I took my car and drove to my daughter's house on Stony Brook Road.
Q: Then what happened?
A: As I saw my son in law, Raymond Heyman, I told him to call the police. He called the police and then he went back to my house.
Q: Then what happened?
A: Raymond, Angela and I went back to my house, in my car. As we came back to the house the police had not arrived yet, and I saw the person that I had seen in my bedroom come walking on the West side of the house, and Raymond talked to him.
Q: Can you describe this person to me?
A: I'll say he was 5'10" or 5'11". Slim looking, short cropped honey colored hair. He had tan pants, and I think he had brown shoes. I could see a pair of blue briefs, as his pants hanging low

on his hips. He had like a polo shirt with a light color, as he came out he took his shirt off, and he started to walk away from the house. I saw Raymond following him away from the house.

Q: I have showed you items in evidence bag # 636190, can you tell me if you recognize this, and if you do, from where?

A: Yes, these items are mine, they were all in my bedroom in different places. I remember especially the Navaho Indian pieces that we bought in Arizona. All the pieces in the bag belongs to me.

Q: How about the items in bag labeled # 640783?

A: All six wrist watches are mine. They were all in my bedroom.

Q: How about the pearls in bag # AA23449?

A: They are mine, they are not real, but they were in my bedroom.

Q: How about the items in bag # 640782?

A: The black pearls, the onyx ring, and on ear ring all belong to me. The four bracelets are also mine, and all these items were in my bedroom.

Q: Bag # AA23448 holds 11 necklaces. Do you recognize these?

A: Yes, I recognize all 11 of them. They came from my bed room.

Q: How about bag # AA23466?

A: The written notes are not mine, the watch is not mine, the cigarettes, lighter and the matches are not mine. The pliers and the "chain" is not mine. The medication, laxative and Bisoprolol/hctz, and the Neosporin are my items. The Bisprolol/hctz was in the kitchen, and the laxative and the Neosporin was in my bathroom.

Q: How about the sunglasses in bag # AA23463, that was found on your roof?

A: I have never seen them before.

Q: How about the toothbrush and the watch in evidence bag # 658019?

A: Yes they are mine, I just bought the toothbrush, I was going to bring it to Virginia Beach. The watch is older. The toothbrush was in my bathroom , and the watch was in my bedroom.

Q: How about the watch in evidence bag # AA 23465, that was found on the lawn on the West side of your house?

A: Yes, that is mine, and it was in my bedroom.

Q: Another watch, in bag # AA23464, that was found on the back steps of your deck?

A: Yes that is mine, and that was also in my bedroom.

Q: Is there anything else you can tell me about this incident?

A: No, not except fro the fact that it was the scare of my life.

Statement ended at 9:50 P.M, and contains two pages.

NOTICE : False statements made herein are punishable as a Class A Misdemeanor pursuant to Section 210.45 of the Penal Law.

Sworn to before me this 20 th.
Day of May, 2004

SIGNATURE OF DEPONENT

SIGNATURE

TITLE

WITNESS

Inv. Tor O. Tryland   09:50 P.M.
NAME OF PERSON TAKING DEPOSITION

I am sorry to say that this person was arrested and was under the influence of his drug habit and ruined his life and that of his family.

There is one thing that I am thankful for that he didn't wake up when I touched him, thinking he was my grandson.

Chapter Twenty Three

More Trouble

March 1 2005

The early start of the New Year, "WHAT WILL IT HOLD NOW"?

Will the comp. board approve the operation? It was a waiting game with them. I was back working and that morning my arthritis in my hands and arms wasn't too bad, after taking the medication.

Today it was going to be a busy day at the school. The students were having their Spirit Games in the afternoon. My schedule was changed that morning and I took two classes for Mr. Schantz and three for Mrs. Bartolotta. They were good classes, good lesson plans, and great students. I didn't mind taking extra classes at the school; I loved talking to the students. It seems that I couldn't do as much work around the house anymore because of my fall.

CATSKILL HIGH SCHOOL

Office of the Principal
CATSKILL SENIOR HIGH SCHOOL

343 West Main Street
CATSKILL, NEW YORK 1
(518) 943-2300

December 5, 1995

Ladies and Gentlemen:

It is with true pleasure that I write this letter of
reference for Tina Gulino. During the past eight years I
have been fortunate enough to get to know Tina as a student
as well as work with her in an educational setting here at
Catskill High School.

As an adjunct instructor at Columbia-Greene Community
College, I had Tina as a student in a computer application
class. Tina's ability to grasp and understand the computer
concepts and applications should be commended. I found her
to be a hard-working dedicated student. Tina was instructed
in the use of two computer programs: First Choice and
MicrosoftWorks. Each time she demonstrated the ability to
use the program effectively, and I am confident she would be
able to transfer these skills to whatever application
program she were to encounter in the future.

I have also been fortunate enough to get to know Tina as a
co-worker here at Catskill High School. During the past
eight years Tina has been a substitute teacher in the
Occupational Education Department. She has demonstrated an
excellent report with students and has been more than
capable of carrying on a lesson.

I am truly pleased to hear that Tina is continuing her
education and am glad to help her in her endeavor. I
believe Tina has the ability and determination to succeed in
whatever direction her education will take her.

Sincerely,

Cathy A. Bartolotta
Department Chair-Occupational Ed.

df

Willy

I have to tell you about Willy. Willy is the most important person in my life at this time. He is like the son I didn't have, who does all the work that Jim would do when he was here. My children have often mentioned that their Dad *where ever he is* sent Willy to me. I truly believe it's true because I could never take care of all the things that need to be done when you own a house. Willy also reminds me of Jim, when I would say I wanted something done, Jim would get it done. If I mention that I like something done, Willy loved to be part of what I wanted done. I have the feeling that he loves my house as much as I do. In the mornings of the months of March to October, Willy comes in for three hours every Sat. and does the mowing, trims the bushes, sometime paints a room, fixes a faucet and takes the leaves away from my Daffodil patch which grows bigger and bigger every year.

I don't think that I could have the house if I didn't have Willy to take care of it. I am so lucky.

(What my dream house looks like now)

Washington Irving Senior Center July of 2005

Washington Irving Senior Center opened up on July 22nd a few weeks before my operation. I remembered the time when the county presented the plans of what the building would look like. I had seen the old building before this; it had looked like an old shack on a hill. The windows were rusted and rotten, bricks were loose and the roof looked like that if there was a rain storm, it would probably leak inside. I expressed my opinion at the county meeting that when the state grants $400,000.00 that we could get a brand new building instead of wasting it on renovations; but that idea was refused by the board and the senior center received renovations, $400,000.00 worth? Hmm... I must admit that they did a nice job on the inside of the building, but I guess they ran out of money to put in a descent parking lot, many people never come to the center because they can't park there; especially when we have club meetings for the Rip Van Winkle and Catskill Senior Fellowship club meetings.

When the Center opened I was still working and didn't get to go to the center very often and most of the time I would sign up for some trips which the club's offered. I was quite busy with my job, doctors and my health.

August of 2005

I waited more than a year and a half before the compensation board approved the operation. When Dr. Perkins described the details of the operation to me, the one thing that really bothered me was the fact that he told me that he was going to put a disc that would come from a cadaver in me. This wasn't the only thing that bothered me. What if my body refused it? What if this disc had

190

something wrong with it? What if this had an emotional gene in its makeup (crazy thoughts, I know)? But then, I thought what my mother used to say... *"It's destiny, what happens in one's life."* I really didn't feel very sure about the operation and my life. I didn't know if I could work after this; if I couldn't do what I loved, I probably would become very depressed. Feeling that convalescence was for seven weeks, supported my feelings of depression; and couldn't go back to work right way.

On August 24 2005 I was operated on my neck and a cervical disk from a cadaver and was put in my spine, and a titanium clamp is holding it in place. I wasn't very happy about it, in fact I was very unhappy about the circumstances that led up to this. I was wired like a Christmas tree during the operation, every finger had a wire on it as well as other parts of my body; I asked "what's with all the wires"? They informed me that during the operation all the wires would let them know where all my nerve endings were. *I had to accept this answer of course, what could I say? It was too late to back out.* Most of the doctor's were telling jokes, reassuring me that I would be fine. But the convalescence was the pits! Seven weeks of torture, a brace on my neck and I could not turn in it at all. I could not sleep except on a lounge chair.

This was the prelude to a long convalescence and the time that I started really thinking of writing my book. This goal was something that was always in the back of my mind. When you reach a certain age you feel free to express how life has treated you; you want to discuss things that were good and bad, but have survived to live another day. Maybe it's to leave a history for your family or maybe it to realize how you reached this age.

The children of today's world may realize that some goals may change, but they have choices. We sometimes have to take the cards that we are dealt with and make things work for you but *it's never too late if you have the courage and challenge to find a way.*

Old age is an adventure that holds no commitment, just what you want to do the rest of your Life.)

Back to Work 2005

Oct 17, Dr. Perkins said that I could wear a soft collar and it also kept me warm since the weather was becoming colder. After being home for seven weeks, I returned to work; I had an English teacher's class, I didn't get the lesson plans from the office until after the first period. This would sometimes happen when the office didn't get the lesson plan the day before. Sometimes I would have to call this teacher to get the lesson plans. The class was great and the students helped me get through the first period, and they were glad to see me back. Being home for seven weeks made me realize that I was back and that I could help some of them with their problems.

There was a particular incident that has stayed in my subconscious all these years. One student came to me in class and showed me his arms. He had been burned with a cigarette on one arm, the word love and the other the word hate. His arms were red and inflamed. I tried not to get upset and told him I think he should go down to see the nurse, so I gave him a pass. I couldn't leave the class and waited until the period was over to go down to see the nurse. The student needed help as soon as possible. The nurse called the mother and she got an appointment for the following week to see a psychiatrist. I saw Ken the next day and he came to see me at another class I had. He opened the door and said, I Love you "Mrs. G ", I said I Love you too Ken and he left. The following day I heard that he hung himself that night. I felt something should have been done that day. He should have been saved.

Chapter Twenty Four

On a Happy Note

February 2 2006

This year started on a happy note. I became a Great Grandmother, Christopher James (named after his Great Grandfather.) He weighed in at 9 lb. 14 oz. He was born on my baby brother Frankie's birthday, February 2, ground hog day. It's ironic that this happened but then some things are meant to be. *I guess my brother, who passed away sent us a new baby to take his place.*

Entry in Journal, C.J. Carbone

I really wanted to be there when you were born, but being close to 82 and couldn't travel alone to Chester. Angela your new Grandmother kept me posted on your every move. It was a long day for you and your mother and father and all the families. I can't wait until I see you Saturday. I didn't have to wait till then, your new grandmother and grandfather decided to come and get me and your great aunt Nancy to see you at the hospital.

Entry in Journal March 15 2006

In March, after all the exciting things that happened last month I had signed up to go on a trip with the "Rips" senior club to a St. Pats Day outing. I really didn't want to go; I wasn't feeling quite normal, after my bout with a sinus infection. I felt like something else was wrong. Went to the eye doctor and he said I have Cataracts in both eyes. The right one was the worst so I made an appointment for operation on March 27 after C. J.'s christening

Entry in Journal, C. J., March 19 2006

Today was my birthday and your Christening Day. I guess it will be the perfect day for you and me. You were baptized in the Church your mother and father were married in. What a wonderful place to be. I guess St. Joseph was looking after us. C.J. you really were uncomfortable in your baptism suit because you cried through the ceremony. Your mother took off your coat and that helped a little. What a blessed day.

We arrived at the restaurant and your mother nursed you and you finally fell asleep in my arms. How blessed I am and hope to talk to you someday soon. I know that you will grow up to be healthy, wealthy and a very wise young man. With a mother and father who will direct you as you grow up, you can't miss.

Eye Operation March 27 2006

My daughter Nancy came with me. The doctor sent a limousine to pick us up at 5:30 in the morning and took us to Albany. The operation only took a couple of hours and then took us back home. Everything went well except the doctor made another appointment for 2weeks later for the other eye. All I could feel was "get this over with!"

I must admit my eyes felt much clearer after the operation. I went back to work in a week, and subbed Ms. N's French class. Her lesson plan called for the class to play French Scrabble. Well, our American student's had a surprise for the French students whom were visiting at that time. Every other year a group of our students would go to France and the next year a group from France would come to our school. One of the French students brought in a French film about a very famous person who was a surfer. I usually stick to the lesson plan but today was different, they were our guests. Knowing that M's N would have approved of it, and the fact of always having taken her classes, she trusted me to do the right thing.

Spring Break 2006

Having new wood floors installed, turned the house into an upside down place; I didn't know where anything was. I could have enjoyed my school break but duty calls. I forced myself to stay home and tackle some of the boxes filled with things that belonged to each room. I started with my bedroom. How did I accumulate so much stuff and I mean stupid stuff, a tag from the dress I wore to my Granddaughter's wedding, a box of stones that I collected in our travel to places with Jim. One white stone from the Island of Capri, my most treasured place. Oh how I wish I could go back there again. What beautiful memories came rushing back, a box of cards of all the places Jim and I had seen in our travels. How luckily we were to travel in our time together. Another box full of cards and things that our daughters made when they were little in school, and cards they made for Jim and me. The bad part about going over the stuff is what to do with all of it, get rid of it? This was going to be a *Big Decision* on my part. I remember what one of my books on Feng Shui said about clutter, it's not good for your psyche so my clutter had to go after sixty years. *My life has got to get simpler. I did try to keep it simple but admit some memories I still needed to keep.*

My Baby Sister's Life May 2, 2006

I received a call from my niece Annie. She received a call from my sister Jean's daughter from Florida, Tina Ann, who was named after me and my sister Anna. My younger sister Jean was in the hospital in ICU, with heart failure, high blood pressure and was diabetic. I asked if I could call her and I did. Jean answered the phone said she was feeling a little better. They are going to keep her there till she is stabilized.

Jeanie was my younger sister and was a rebel all her life. When she was in school she was considered a "Tom Boy". Sports were her passion: tennis, basketball, and a few others. When she graduated High School she received a scholarship to Connell University in New York State. We were all very proud of her accomplishment but she had to leave home. At the time there wasn't very much money to send her to college. The whole family wanted her to go so we all worked so that my parents could afford the extra tuition. My sister Anna and I gave her some of our clothes. Most of the time she would go into closet when we went to work. We always knew she borrowed the clothes because she would use them when she played her games. She always denied that she wore them. We loved her and always wanted her to succeed.

The first year at college she met her first husband. When my father found out he went to the college and asked her to come home. She refused and dad came home disappointed. The rest of the family felt the same way.

My sister did eventually come home and had a very troubled marriage and got a divorce after having four children. She worked all her life; she smoked, and was married three times and lost a son and three husbands. She didn't take care of herself.

I had lent her my trunk that grandmother Vitina left me when she passed away. I loved that trunk and had papered the inside with wallpaper with roses on a white background. I kept my personal items in it and had so many memories of my life with my grandmother. My sister never gave it back to me and I never asked her for it. At this time in my life a trunk doesn't matter, because my little sister passed on May 5 2006 with her children at her side.

Memorial Weekend May 27–29 2006

It appeared that everyone came up this weekend. My sister Ann was up from the city to open up their summer house. My extended Sicilian families also were up. They haven't been up all winter, only their children would come up to ski.

Sat. the 27th we had an engagement BBQ party at my Grandson's Tom's house. It was an invitation for Susan's family, his fiancée, our family and his friends to meet before the wedding. His sister Tina and Chris and baby C.J. came up from Chester NY. It was a beautiful day and we ate all day.

On Sunday the 28th it was a special day that answered some questions that had bothered me most of my life. In the morning I went down the hill to see my extended Sicilian family, I felt that I hadn't seen them in a year. We caught up with the things that happened during the winter. Our conversation always came about the old country and the old habits that were left behind.

I thought I knew about my Sicilian customs but I found out about some things that never were told to me. At this late time in my life they say you learn something new every day. What I learned this year was a question that I should have known the answer to when I was sixteen, when my mother said she was never going to heaven if she died.

We talked about our mothers and how hard their lives were in the old country, how many children they had there. It wasn't their choice and caused a hardship on the family. Some of the women had their remedies of having an abortion. I had mentioned to Josephine that my Mother was pregnant a month before my wedding and had purchased a bunch of long stem Italian parsley, which she never used for cooking.

Josephine was born in the old country and knew what the women did to bring on an abortion. She also said it was against the law and also against their religion, and that many women died of infection from using the parsley for abortion. Most women didn't go to a doctor for fear of the law and their priests. All totaled, my mother aborted six of her pregnancies and was very lucky, but the last pregnancy she had to go to the hospital.

This was always the question that I never received the answer to until now. How guilty she felt all her of life, even at my wedding she insisted that she wear a black dress to mourn her abortions. God had his reason for my mother not remembering anything that happened in her married life. At the end of her life she developed Alzheimer's and never remembered anything about her life and I became her mother.

(My Mother)

After Memorial Weekend Sunday June 4 2006

I had a surprise phone call. It was about nine thirty in the morning. I picked it up and on the other end came the voice of my Goddaughter Angela and her husband Jiggs, her grandson and my nephew Jim and the rest of her family from Florida. They were in the New York City and wanted to pass to see us on their way to my nephew Jim's house on Saranac Lake.

There was no question that I wanted to see them and so did the rest of the family. My daughters had not seen their cousins in nineteen years. Everyone was scattered all over the country and it made it hard to get together.

There was one thing I had to do first, cancel my dinner date. They were more important than any dinner date that I had that day. I wanted them to stay for Lunch. It takes about two and half hours to get to Palenville from the New York City so that gave me enough time to make lunch.

We had so much to talk about, the old times, when we were together at our house for the holidays. They remembered our Thanksgivings and who wanted the drumsticks first. It brought back memories of their father Sal when he would make all the children laugh, especially if he had a few glasses of wine. It was such a wonderful day and our love for each other never waned. We promised that if we could that someday we would get together again.

June 2006 Interview for a New Superintendent

Before the school year ended in June, I was asked to attend an interview for a new superintendent. This was a serious assignment I had never done before. I felt that my choice meant that the person would have to prove themselves within three years to get tenure. There were four applicants applying for the Job. My choice was a person that had experience running a school in a fairly large district. The other interviewers must have the same though, because Dr. Kate Farrell became our superintendent. I must admit I was a little apprehensive; would she be another administrator who would make drastic changes?

September's new semester was a busy time and I was subbing about fifteen days a month and things were going great. In the end of January of the New Year I was planning to go on vacation the week the school had regents. It was going to be my great grandson's first birthday on February 2nd in Myrtle Beach, South Carolina. I went down and came back February 6th of 2007.

Chapter Twenty Five

Big Changes, Laid Off from Work

January 2007

Another new administration and I assumed that I was going to be called. It was now toward the end of February and wondered why I was not called. I decided to call Jeff Elliott, Coordinator, and Substitute Calling Service whom was in charge of Sub Finder and asked what was happening and why I wasn't called. He told me that I made 58 days of subbing from September of 06 to one week in January and was only allowed 40 days. I had to be laid off because I was not certified by the state. I was told that I could work in another school for 40 days. For nineteen years that I was there this law was never applied to subs. Evidently getting subs was always a problem in most schools so therefore the law was never enforced. *Maybe this law should be changed in some way.*

Someone from the administration said, write to the Department of Education and explain my problem. I did write a letter and received a thank you letter for being a good sub all those years; when I started subbing there were no requirements for certification.

Having an A. S. Degree from LaGuardia Community College and working in Richmond Hill High School as a full time Para professional, I had my own program in charge of Special Education students. Catskill School District thought that I was exceptional as a teacher in March 22 1988.

My feelings now are why should I go back to school after I received my BA in 2001 at University of New Paltz? Anyway I don't think going 80 miles back and forth at my age was a good idea especially in the winter, *done that already.*

The education and experience in my nineteen years is worth more than any piece of paper. At my age and my life experiences as a substitute teacher, a mother, grandmother and great grandmother, I gave all the students the emotional, empathy, and love that they needed at their age. My expertise in all those years that I enjoyed being with the students for the five generations, gave me hope for our children. I accepted the ruling and worked with Dr. Farrell in getting the word out for the School Budget for the year. I even made a T V commercial for the budget, *which passed.*

Took My Name off the Sub List March 19 2007

I gave myself a birthday present today at age 83. It wasn't materialistic, but it did make a difference in my life. What I wrote in my journal on that day.

Why do I always have to struggle for what I want? Maybe it's because I am being tested or maybe someone up there is testing me to see how the system works? Could be I am learning as I go along; who Knows?

I have so much to be thankful for, but sometimes I wish for a bit more luck. Working all my Life, having made some foolish moves, let some opportunities pass me by, because I had commitments to my family. Well, I can't do anything about it. *Maybe I am tired of struggling. I guess I am depressed today!*

Coming to the conclusion of what has been happening in the last few months, it needed to be addressed. I felt that I didn't want to go back to New Paltz to get my Masters. It was a big decision but it was time, I called Jeff at Sub Finder and told him to take my name off the top of the list, this was in August of 07 he was disappointed and said he didn't know where he would get a good sub to take my place.

My life hasn't ended with any regrets and not a day goes by when I see one or more of the students and their families. They give me a hug and their love is worth all the years that I worked with them.

My next goal is to write about my life. After leaving my fifth career in August I realized that I was free to do whatever I wanted. My goal was now fresh in my mind, MY BOOK.

Volunteer at the Senior Center 2007

I was going almost every day to the Washington Irving Senior Center and volunteered in the kitchen for the Department of the Aging. They have a program of making meals for the home bound seniors. I would go there at 8.30AM and help Tezera and Martha prepare the food for the day. They also would serve lunch for any one that came to the Center. We would work all morning and I would get done about 10:30 a.m. Why not use the rest of the morning on starting my book. I could have used the computers at the center but I needed a place that was secure and quiet. I bought myself a laptop and found a place in the dining room and it. I would work until 12:00 when the hot food came in. I then would go on the assembly line in charge of how many lunches had to go out. This didn't last very long and much to my regret, I always felt that Tezera was going to get a promotion which she deserved. *Everything changed when* she left in July 2008. She sometimes comes into the kitchen to visit and she is quite busy and is doing a terrific job.

The Passing of My Sister Anna July 12, 2007

My sister and I were only18 months apart. At one point she was my little sister, whom I took care of most of her life.

We were always together growing up and in our adult life we were inseparable. We always knew how we felt when things were good or bad. She had the most beautiful voice and a heart of gold. I remember always sleeping with her in an old iron bed, and I told her that someday I would buy a new bed room set. That dream came true when I first went to work at 18. What I bought was a Maple bed room set and paid $2.00 a week and paid it off. We had the set until we both got married and then I gave it to our baby sister Jean. Ann was the introvert and always was satisfied with *Status Quo.* I was the extrovert I always was challenged to try something new and work hard to make it come true.

We both got married almost a year apart. Jim and I got married on April, 8 1945 and Ann and Ben were married March 2 1946.

Her life didn't start out very nice in the beginning. The person that she married who from the first day *criticized her thought and every move.* Their first meal that she made, he told her that it was disgusting and that she didn't know how to cook. She cried on her honeymoon. As time went on things didn't get any better, when she bought something she had to give him a receipt of how much she spent.

One time when she sprained her ankle we went to the Pharmacy for a container of Epson salt to bathe her ankle. When I came out of the store she asked me for the receipt. I knew the pharmacist since I was young and I didn't want to ask him for a receipt. I told Ann to tell her husband I gave the box of Epson salt; I couldn't believe that my sister's marriage was in trouble.

What happened next was the most tragic episode of her life, the death of her first born child in 1948. I can't recall on the day it happen except that she was almost 2 years old, a beautiful child named Angela. She had the same name as my daughter who was three years old then. I was home when her husband called to tell me that they lost their daughter. He didn't explain what happened and all I could think of was, go find her and where is my sister. He said she was upset and couldn't talk to me. I never got the whole story and only as my mother told me years later. They went to a park in Staten Island and he was holding his daughter and my sister was rowing a boat on the pond. She slipped out of his arms and went overboard and sank to the bottom of the pond. My sister went in and tried to find her but the water was too murky and they couldn't find her. The pond had to be drained in order to find her.

My sister never told me what happened and I never asked. Most of her married life from then on and until 61 years later was always with remorse and constant complaining about her life and she would always say she wanted to die. In all those years she would tell me about her husband and how he would control her. He would say stupid things, like don't run the water, don't flush the toilet, and don't run the dish washer because it would use hot water. When he retired and when it came to food he never wanted to eat hers. He cooked and ate different food, mostly beans, garlic and fish. The only time he ate meat or chicken was if it was free, or when he went to someone's house or a party. I could go on and on with his idiosyncrasies. *I often wondered how did she put up with a person like that all her life?*

There was a time when her children were all in school she said she wanted to go to work, so she got a part time job as bookkeeper for a real estate firm. His first words were he wanted her pay check. I told her give him some of the money and save some for herself in her daughter's name.

July 12 2007

I received a call from my sister's daughters, Nancy and Annie from down state in Queens, New York, they were taking my sister to the hospital. They said she couldn't walk and had difficulty breathing. Ann was living alone in her Condo in Howard Beach near her daughters. She couldn't stand living with this man more than a week and she would have anxiety attacks every time she came to her house upstate.

She was in one hospital and within the month they found that she had Lung Cancer *she never smoked but had* second *hand smoke* and had to transfer to a Hospice. They also said they couldn't operate; it had spread thru out her body. They didn't give her much hope. I wanted to be with her but I had not traveled downstate in 15 years and my children refused to let me go alone. So I had to wait till Angela and Ray took me down. I did call and

210

most of the time I spoke to her nurse. On Sunday she told me that Ann had a good day, she went to Mass in the morning and ate her lunch, she even smiled. When I talked to my sister she said, she wasn't feeling well and that she couldn't breathe and her feet were swollen and she couldn't walk. It seemed to me she had good and bad days.

August 12 2007

It was 7:45 PM and Luddy, my Godson who is also my sister's only son, called. It was the phone call that I knew was going to happen. He didn't say anything except that he took her down stairs in the wheelchair yesterday for some fresh air and she was happy. I told him that I was glad he was with her when she passed. She could always count on him, and her young daughter Annie whom would travel from Long Island to Queens almost every day. She would always make her mother laugh and smile.

When I saw my sister in the casket I didn't recognize her. In one month she had lost so much weight and her face looked as if she had suffered so badly. My family and I went downstate to Howard Beach for the Funeral. They had a Mass and the Priest gave a good sermon, he really made you feel that there is life after death.

We all went to lunch at a local restaurant. My grandchildren met my Godson's children which they had never met, and greeted each other as if they knew each other all their lives. They took pictures with each other and promised to see one another again. My feeling about my sister's death is still something I can't accept Yet! I regret that I wasn't with her when she needed me. This is one of her letters that she wrote when she was overwhelmed with anxiety.

Dear Tina,

I couldn't ask for a better sister than you. You always seem to know just exactly what to say to me to keep me on the straight and narrow path when anxiety takes over my life.

I admire your enthusiasm and spontaniety in all you do. You have a natural creative talent and use it for the good of all the people around you.

May "God Bless you" with "Good health" for a "lifetime".

Merry Christmas

Love always,
Your sister,
Anna

Thank you for a wonderful birthday.
OXOXOX

Picture of Our Communion.

Picture before Anna passed away.

Senior Center October 2007

When I signed off from the Substitute List of Catskill High School, I got involved in the Senior Center. Emotionally I needed to keep busy after my sister's passing.

Ann Marie is the Director of the center and Cressa, Assistant Director and Celeste whom keeps the Center spic & span. They are the ones that made sure that we all become creative and busy. There is something going on every day at the Center: Camera Club, Exercise Class, Weight Watchers, and Wii Bowling.

Most of the times I was working on the book and didn't take advantage of all the other things that were available. I did join the bowling league however because I had never bowled and I felt it was a challenge. At the end of the bowing league my partner and I came in sixth.

A Halloween Party at the Center

I was free now to do what I wanted. No more commitments. We were asked to dress up for the party. I couldn't think of what I would go as. I remembered that Ray whom was a chef had a white coat and hat, which he had kept after he had retired, it was perfect. After all, I was a chef extraordinaire after cooking all my life for the family and all the holidays.

In the picture I won first prize for originality. Most of us take our parties very seriously. We have most all the members dress up and many make their own costumes. There is always a party at the center and we really have a lot of fun.

(That's me 4th from the left in a chef suit!)

Fellowship Follies October 8, 2007

Rosemarie Graham a retired English teacher from Catskill High School wrote a play called "The Fellowship Follies." She became the director of the play and most of us joined in the adventure. We would all have a part in the play. Mine was Patty of the "Andrew Sisters". What fun to try and lip sync the words of the song "Don't sit under the Apple Tree". I was told that I was the middle person and had to lip sync one part all alone. It took us about a month of rehearsing and we finally put on the play on October 18, 2007 at our meeting. We had advertised the play and there was quite a crowd. It was scary to perform to such a crowd. Peggy Kreitner and Jo Payne were the other sisters. I must say it was a lot of fun to put on the play. Rose Marie was a pro, for she had always helped to put on our school plays.

The Catskill Senior Fellowship Club

presents

the Second

Fellowship Follies

October 18, 2007

Washington Irving
Senior Center, Catskill

Interview by Inez Dickens October 22, 2007

October was a very busy and fun month. I was also interviewed by Inez Dickens for her column "Cancer Kicking Warriors" written for the Daily Mail. Her column is about women who had cancer and survived it.

NEWS   Monday, October 22, 2007

Cancer Kickin' Warriors
A woman who didn't let cancer stop her

By Inez Dickens and Roberta Saniga

Dear Heroes and Heroines,

Recently, I had the pleasure of meeting a woman who was so positive, upbeat and vivacious she inspired me. This inspiring lady is Tina Gulino. For those of you who live in the area, the name may be very familiar to you. Gulino was a substitute teacher for the Catskill High School for 19 years before retiring last year.

Prior to this, Gulino worked for the New York City school system. Her love and devotion for children caused her to set up a program for special education children. In her program, she taught them the food preparation trade. She held class once a week and then they were aloud to test their skills by working in the cafeteria.

Gulino and her husband traveled extensively until 1995, when he passed away.

In 1998, through self-examination, Gulino noticed a lump about the size of a pea on her left breast. She immediately went to the doctor who performed a needle biopsy on her. She heard the words we all love to hate — she had breast cancer! Due to its size, approximately 1.5cm, Gulino had the option of getting a lumpectomy. Because she lost her beloved father to lung cancer, she said she would not rest unless she got it all out so she opted for a mastectomy. Her primary doctor agreed with her.

She was scheduled to go in for surgery in May. But as fate would have it, her appendix ruptured and she ended up with a different surgery — appendectomy. Her recovery period for this was May 23 to July 2.

In July, she had her mastectomy and this feisty woman by her own choice only stayed in the hospital overnight.

Throughout this time Gulino had the love and support of her two daughters and loving friends.

What amazed me the most about this woman was her attitude about her ordeal with cancer. She, like most of us when diagnosed, thought she was going to die. She asked her doctor, "how long do I have?" He said, "I don't know." Her response was, "Good, then I'm going back to college!" And that's just what she did. In 2001, this mother and grandmother of two got her degree in communications and media!

That year she was celebrated as one of the oldest people to get their degree.

Gulino's message is if you got cancer, get rid of it. She said she's done for everyone else, now she's going to do for herself. Cancer was not going to stop her. She told me her one goal, which she will fulfill, is to write a book. Her message is "be positive, life does go on after cancer."

As you can guess, her attitude has inspired many people. She lives the message that you can do whatever you want, no matter what obstacles are thrown at you. It's all in the attitude.

Tina Gulino we want to thank you for inspiring us and touching so many people. I know your former students are especially proud of you. And folks I can tell you this is a beautiful woman with a golden heart. You are our Heroine of the Week!

Please e-mail your stories to cancerkickinwarriors@yahoo.com

I was happy to tell her about my adversity with Cancer, and my attitude, that made me conquer it.

Matthew Connor Heyman February 14 2008

Born the year of the Rat [Chinese calendar], born in a leap year at 8:03pm. He weighed 6lbs 3 ounces. He is an Aquarius.

Now I have two great grandsons that are Aquarius. Received a call at 8:45 from my daughter Angela she said everything went well. They had arrived at the hospital at 5 am on February14 2008.

Thomas was there with Susan and her mother as well as Angela and Ray. I remember when Thomas was born and now he was becoming a father; where did the time go?

I guess Matthew, I will see you soon. I can't wait.

To think, that my baby brother Frankie, born on February 2 1940 who left this earth on February 14 2005, sent us another little boy on this day 66 years later.

Maybe it was written or maybe it is destiny that my brother wherever he is, knows that he will always be remembered for the rest of our lives.

Chapter Twenty Six

A New Part of My Life

June 2008

We came down to Myrtle Beach on June 18th. Angela, Ray and I started out at 5:30 in the morning from Catskill; the trip was great. We did it one day only, stopping for an hour to rest. Ray drove most of the day and Angela drove when we got to South Carolina and continued till the end of the trip. We arrived at 7:30 in the evening and went to Tina and Chris's new house. They were overwhelmed with all the boxes they had, and so were we. They had just moved in that day. Where do you start first? Which room? This was going to take months to get things in place. With all of us helping we finally made some headway.

South Carolina is starting to grow on me. There are many pluses to living here and few minuses. I guess you get used to change. I am staying at Ray and Angie's condo and am getting to like my leisure living. One of the pluses is that my granddaughter Tina is having another baby now. I'll be a great grandmother again and that will make three great grandchildren: Christopher James, Matthew Connor, and the new baby's name will be Gabriella Maria.

(From Left, Christopher James, Matthew Connor, and Gabriella Marie)

My New Name, "GiGi" Great Grandmother.

A Great Granddaughter September 2008

In September 15 2008 Gabriella Maria Carbone was born. She weighed 7 pound 7 oz. Her mother Tina and father Chris were happy she was finally born by Caesarean birth. Angela and Ray and C J were there and they waited till Gabriella came into the world. A month later, C J asked his mother if she could put her back in her tummy. He was 2 1/2 years old at that time but now he is four and her big brother learned to accept her.

October 2008

The year is almost over, and we are going to have an election in November. I have been though many years of elections, but this is the most disgusting one I have seen on TV. We are in a recession and people are hurting. Many have lost their jobs and their homes. I remember in 2000 when I was working in the school as a sub, Mr. T McKay, the Spanish teacher, said that if President Bush came in he would destroy America. I didn't think that any one person could do this but he did, as we know now. What I do know is that being born during the Depression, how it was growing up at that time. It was greens, vegetables, and beans. In the many years of my life I have always remembered how hard it was for us children and for my parents to survive and come though the hard times. *Now times are different in this day and age and there are so many more modern wants that are available to our children than we can keep up with. Finally for all the new stuff that is presented to us every day, many mothers' are working to keep up with the new times.* For the children of today it's a new way of living. Their wants are never ending. I believe in progress but when new things are on the market every week, and yet are obsolete the next week, our children still want the new stuff, it isn't progress. We must make them understand that some things will not be available to them in the future unless they are educated and they really truly want to have the good things in life. I'm neither a Republican nor Democrat, but what I have lived through, it doesn't matter. I still watch my pennies and plan my goal. Some come to fruition, but some have to change to *survive*. With my attitude about life I will survive.

Gabby's Christening November 2008

The family is looking forward to Gabriela Marie Carbone's (we call her Gabby for short) christening. We are all going down to Newburgh to the church where Tina and Chris were married. They came up from South Carolina so that she can be christened in the same church. Deacon Peter officiated the christening and did a beautiful ceremony. Gabby didn't even cry; she slept through the whole ceremony. After it, we went to Union Square for lunch. We were quite a crowd. It was a beautiful day that will be remembered forever. At my time in life I treasure all my memories.

November 12, 2008

My great grandson CJ (Christopher James) and I spent the whole day yesterday with each other. He and I had a good time together. We painted with watercolor and I had a better time than he did. His grandmother, my daughter Angela, was very busy getting ready to close the house in Palenville for the winter. Ray and Angela have a condo in South Carolina which they go to in the winter. They became snowbirds in 2007 and their daughter Tina lives there permanently.

I am thinking that maybe I would like to go down to South Carolina in the winter. The winter is becoming a problem. The fuel bill is almost $4,000 for the year, and the snow is a problem too. I remember that I could always shovel the snow, but now with my arthritis and all the other afflictions that I have it's too much to do.

Christmas 2008

I am a member of the two clubs that meet at the center; the Catskill Fellowship and the Rip Van Winkle Seniors. This year the RIPS had a special event at the Christmas banquet. The president, Werner and his wife Lynne Knudsen put on a play at the dinner. Rudolph the red nosed reindeer, as well as Santa's other reindeer came in pulling a sled with Santa and Mrs. Claus who handed out presents for everyone. The reindeer were members all dressed up with antlers on their heads. It was a surprise of course. I got to play Cupid, one of Santa's special reindeer. Even though we were all seniors, we really enjoyed Christmas that day.

Chapter Twenty Seven

My Purse Stolen from My Porch

January 12 2009

I wanted to end this book in 2008 but it seems that faith had another agenda for me to go through. It was the date January 12th, and the birthday of my oldest, daughter Angela. I woke up early that morning and decided to go shopping. Angela and Ray were in Myrtle Beach and we had talked on the phone. I would keep them posted on what I planned on doing for the day.

When I came home from shopping in Kingston I realized I had quite a few bundles to take into the house. I stopped the car near the porch stairs, and put all the bundles on it. I had frozen food so I took them into the house first. While inside I received a call and was on the phone about 10 minutes. After the call I went out to get the rest of the food, I remembered I had left my purse with the bags on the porch, but now it wasn't there. That's when I panicked and didn't know what to do first. Who could have taken it? I called my grandson Jim and we went through the house. He thought maybe I had put it somewhere in the house and didn't remember where. I thought I was losing my mind. I knew it was with the other groceries. Now, I had to do something because I had many personal items, such as health documents, license and credit cards in my purse. I called 911 and got the state troopers who said they would come over right away and searched the house. I felt they were treating me as if I was going senile because of my age. They even looked in my fridge. I may have lost some of my memory but I don't think I've lost it all. I thought about it and then called the bank and explained what happened. I told them to look for any checks after a certain check number. Actually the bank called me when a man came in to cash a $2,500 check supposedly signed by me. I told the bank to call the police. The police came to the bank and got a picture that was taken of the man who tried to cash the check as well as a description of the car that he was driving. The police caught the driver of the car but never recovered my purse. What hurt the most was the picture of my great grandchildren, my husband's last picture. Most of all was a dollar bill that my husband carried throughout World War II, he gave it to me and I carried it with me for the past 14 years. I still haven't heard anything else from them.

I guess there is a saying that God gives us only problems that we can handle. This is only the first one for this year. I hope the rest of the year will be better.

MV-78B (8/05)

New York State Department of Motor Vehicles

REPORT OF LOST, STOLEN OR CONFISCATED MOTOR VEHICLES ITEMS

Please read the information on the back of this form.

The following item(s) have been reported:
☐ Lost ☒ Stolen/destroyed as result of a crime
☐ Confiscated or surrendered to police to comply with S/R order

☒ Driver License ☐ Non-Driver ID ☐ Learner Permit
☐ License Plate(s) ☐ Registration/Sticker

Number of Plates Lost, Stolen or Confiscated: ☐ One ☐ Two	Plate Number/License or Client ID Number ▮▮▮▮	Type of Registration/License Class D	Expiration Date 3/19/11	Date Reported to Police 1/12/09

Name of Licensee/Registrant	Gulino, Tina

Address of Licensee/Registrant	11 Stony Brook Ext Palenville, NY 12463

Police Agency NYSP	Agency/Precinct Address SP Coxsachie	Case Number 2854094

Signature of Officer ♦ Tfr ▮▮▮▮	Rank & Shield or Tax I.D. No. 1256	Date 1/12/09

Tfr. Ahrberg

SUPPORTING DEPOSITION (CPL §100.20)

NEW YORK STATE POLICE

PAGE 1 OF 1

THE PEOPLE OF THE STATE OF NEW YORK
-- vs.
Defendant(s)

INCIDENT LOCATION:	LOCATION OF DEPOSITION:
STATE OF NEW YORK *LOCAL CRIMINAL* COURT	STATE OF NEW YORK
COUNTY OF *GREENE*	COUNTY OF *GREENE*
TOWN OF *CATSKILL*	TOWN OF *CATSKILL*

DATE On 01/20/2009	TIME STARTED AT PM	Full Name: t, TINA J GULINO

State The Following:

ON 01/20/09, A NEW YORK STATE TROOPER CAME TO MY HOUSE WITH A PHOTOCOPY OF TWO CHECKS THAT WERE STOLEN FROM MY ACCOUNT. THEY WERE CHECKS FROM TRUSTCO BANK, CHECK N▮▮ ▮▮0978 AND 0982. THEY WERE BOTH FILLED OUT TO CASH AND MY NAME WAS SIGNED ON THE BOTTOM ▮▮ CHECKS. NEITHER THE HANDWRITING ON THE CHECKS, OR THE SIGNATURE OF MY NAME ON THE CHE▮ ▮ IN MY HANDWRITING. I DID NOT FILL OUT THESE CHECKS, AND GAVE NO PERSON PERMISSION TO F▮ ▮HEM OUT. I ALSO GAVE NO PERSON PERMISSION TO SIGN MY NAME TO ANY OF THE CHECKS.

February 12ᵗʰ 2009

We are having a RIPS meeting Thursday. This is a special meeting. It's Lynn's *"baby"*. She's always thinking of special events for each meeting, this one is Mardi Gras. Most of us started to make the event real. I think she stayed up nights thinking how to make her dream come true. I remember when she was a nurse in Catskill High School she was dedicated to the students and didn't have time to fantasize about fun things like this. We worked on making this party for the past 5 days. It was wonderful that so many of the seniors participated in her fantasy, and it came alive. Everyone was interested and worked together to make it come true. I was also surprised how many dressed for the occasion. It reminded me of how we were when we were young. We didn't have fantasies only fun. I may be wrong but at this time in my life there are no more fantasies only the hope of another day.

April 20th 2009

Angela and Ray were still down in Myrtle Beach for the winter. The last winter of 2008 in Catskill was long and cold. Every other day we had snow or rain that turned into ice. It was kind of depressing when I talked to Angela on the phone they said I should go down for a change. The question was... could I go down by myself. Angela said "yes" and made arrangements for my flight down one way. They were coming up north after staying down all winter. I really wanted to see my great-grandchildren, so I agreed to go and ride back home with them. Joe and Nancy took me to Albany International Airport and I flew with US Air to Charlotte, NC. The flight down was great. I landed in Charlotte, NC and took another plane to Myrtle Beach. There were nonstop flights from LaGuardia, but I had no way to get down there. It would take almost three hours to get to LaGuardia from Palenville and my flight from Albany only took 4 hours total. I arrived at noon; it felt great to travel again. I was apprehensive about going alone but everyone at the airport was great. I wasn't worried and I think from now on I'll fly down. The family was waiting for me and took me to lunch.

I was down there from April 20th till May 6th. While I was there my Arthritis wasn't as bad as during the winter upstate. I didn't have any pain in my knees nor hands, and could pick up my great grandchildren, CJ and Gabriella. On that trip to Myrtle Beach something happened. That was the first time I made a decision that fast. I was set to live in Palenville for the rest of my life, even though it costs $4,000 a year for fuel. There was a Condo for sale, and with a little persuasion from my kids they talked me into looking at it. It was right across the pond from where Angela and Ray's Condo is. They had bought their Condo when Tina and Chris moved to Myrtle Beach in 2006. After many pros and cons, they convinced me that I would save my $4,000 if I went to Myrtle Beach in the winter and closed up my house in Palenville. What I thought their reasoning was because they wanted me away from the snow and ice of an upstate winter.

What was I doing at my age investing in a Condo? This was the ultimate challenge, my friend Jo said, "I didn't realize you were 85 years old, and how could you take on such a financial endeavor." Maybe she was right; I did realize that it could be an investment for my two daughters after I am gone.

May 2009

We weren't home about a week when, believe it or not, I came down with the worse case of Shingles. I think that in my lifetime I've never said I wanted to die. I think that only someone who has had shingles knows the excruciating pain, and the invasion of your body. My girlfriend Jo had it, but hers was a mild case. When I spoke to my doctor he warned me that it may stay in my system for a very long time. I hope not.

My Other Neighbors on My Road September 16th 2009

On my road, my neighbors have always been a place of trust and tranquility. When the Schanley's would go away we would tell each other to watch the house. We would exchange plants, food items; fresh strawberries, cookies that Cindy baked and she would stop to see how I was. I have seen most of their children Tom, Amanda and my Alaina grow up to be beautiful adults. I had most of them in class at Catskill High when they were young. To me they were my children.

Well today two of my other neighbors gave me a gift. My dear friend Helga, who I've known eleven years, said she wanted to spruce up my car. She wanted to make sure it was cleaned up to take down to Myrtle Beach. We usually go out shopping and have lunch together. She came to America 48 years ago during WWII. She has three grown sons and just became a widow.

Then there is Rusty and Diane, who I've known forever since I first came to live on Stony Brook Extension Rd. He wanted to take some scratches off my fender. When I got the car back it turned out just like it was new again. How do I thank them? He would also start my car in the winter when I had to go to work at the school. I didn't refuse the offer, being that I have Arthritis in my hands. I had their son Anthony in my classes. He is now a pharmacist and lives in Florida.

I Became a Snow Bird October 10 2009

I will be leaving for Myrtle Beach on the 10th of the month. Ray and Angie will be driving down with my car, this gave me the possibility to bring more things that I will need down at the Condo. I took a night flight from Albany at seven PM and arrived in Myrtle Beach at eleven PM. Chris was at the airport and picked me up. It was a long day when I arrived at the Condo and there were boxes that had to opened, but I went straight to bed. Tomorrow is another day. Angela and Ray arrived the next day, with more boxes. I had planned to really work on my book but the best plans were beyond my control and made it impossible to do.

Myrtle Beach December 2009

I have been in Myrtle Beach for two months; felt that I am in another world here. The pace of life is much slower than that up in New York. It sort of reminds me of some of the European countries that Jim and I visited. Now I have more time to think of my life and what I look forward to. Myrtle Beach has given me a new perspective of what I want to do with the rest of my life.

I never had time to just sit and enjoy a quiet time and remember the times I didn't have enough time for my children. I had always thought that I should have spent more time with them.

Now I have time to see two of my great grandchildren Christopher James and Gabrielle every day. What a Joy to see them grow every day. I wonder what life has in store for them. What will they become in this uncertain future?

My older grandchildren whom are in their 30's and 40's expect me to live till, hundred years old. It would be great, but only God knows the answer to that question. Where did the years go? How did I really reach this age? I blame it on my genetics but I still take one day at a time.

My book is ending, but for now it's time to make my Sicilian dessert for the Holidays. If you have time, try this Sicilian recipe:

Pignolater or Honey Balls

4 to 5 cups of all purpose flour

2 tsp baking power

6 eggs beaten

2 tsp vanilla exact

½ cup white sugar

½ tsp salt

¼ cup canola oil

1½ cup Honey plus ¼ cup light brown sugar

¾ cup pine nuts

Candy sprinkles

Pure Canola Oil

In a large bowl mix together, flour, white sugar, salt, baking powder, make a well in the middle drop in the eggs, vanilla and canola oil. Knead with your hands until the dough leaves the side of bowl and isn't sticky anymore.

Break off pieces of dough and roll it like a pencil then cut

½ inch pieces roll into little balls. Set on a clean dish cloth and cover (so they don't dry out until ready to fry).

In a deep frying pan heat pure canola oil about 2 inches deep. Fry balls until golden brown. Drain on paper towels.

In a large saucepan over medina heat honey and

Brown sugar, bring to a boil about 5 minutes before adding the balls use slotted spoon to remove them to a tray, stack the ball like a Christmas tree. Sprinkle evenly with pine nuts and colored sprinkles, optional chocolate bits.

Delizios

A Written Voice

How complex we humans are to think that reading someone memories, brings back some happy thoughts of their life. Memories are things that have happened and are kept in our subconscious, but when released come flowing back to tell it all. What fun to write about mine, maybe I will have time to write another book or maybe go back to my other hobbies, sewing crafts', painting with water color or make Holiday cookies.

April 23, 2010 A little Foot Note

I am leaving Myrtle Beach for now and going back to my home in Palenville, New York. My arthritis is better and it's time to go back to my mountains. I came to the realization that I have the best of two worlds.

Another Foot Note

Great Grandson Zackary David Heyman

JUNE 28 2010 7 LB. 5 OZ.

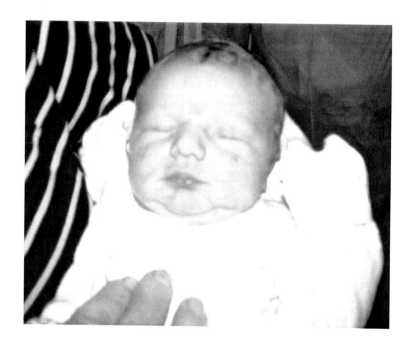

CIAO